Simply Rich

LIFE *and* LESSONS *from the* COFOUNDER *of* AMWAY

A Memoir

Rich DeVos

HOWARD BOOKS
A Division of Simon & Schuster, Inc.
New York   Nashville   London   Toronto   Sydney   New Delhi

Howard Books
A Division of Simon & Schuster, Inc.
1230 Avenue of the Americas
New York, NY 10020

First Howard Books hardcover edition April 2014

HOWARD and colophon are trademarks of Simon & Schuster, Inc.

For information about special discounts for bulk purchases,
please contact Simon & Schuster Special Sales at 1-866-506-1949
or business@simonandschuster.com.

The Simon & Schuster Speakers Bureau can bring authors to your live event.
For more information or to book an event, contact the Simon & Schuster Speakers
Bureau at 1-866-248-3049 or visit our website at www.simonspeakers.com.

Interior design by Davina Mock-Maniscalco
Jacket design by Bruce Gore
Jacket photographs courtesy of the author

Manufactured in the United States of America

10 9 8 7 6 5 4 3 2 1

Library of Congress Cataloging-in-Publication Data

DeVos, Richard M.
  Simply rich: life and lessons from the cofounder of Amway : a memoir / Rich deVos.
    pages cm
1. Amway Corporation—History. 2. DeVos, Richard M. 3. Businessmen—United
States—Biography. I. Title.
  HF5439.H82D48 2014
  381'.142092—dc23
  [B]
                          2013037271

ISBN 978-1-4767-5177-1
ISBN 978-1-4767-5178-8 (ebook)

I dedicate this book to my wife, Helen, who was an integral part of it. None of it would have happened without her love, patience, and encouragement.

CONTENTS

Acknowledgments   ix

Introduction   xi

PART ONE: ACTION, ATTITUDE, AND ATMOSPHERE

CHAPTER ONE   Growing in the Right Atmosphere   1

CHAPTER TWO   Starting a Lifelong Partnership   27

CHAPTER THREE   Try or Cry   47

CHAPTER FOUR   People Helping People to Help
                  Themselves   71

PART TWO: SELLING AMERICA

CHAPTER FIVE   The American Way   91

CHAPTER SIX   Powered by People   107

Contents

CHAPTER SEVEN   The Critics Weigh In   125

CHAPTER EIGHT   Exporting the American Way
                     Worldwide   141

CHAPTER NINE   Finding My Voice   155

CHAPTER TEN   A Magic Moment   169

PART THREE: LIFE ENRICHER

CHAPTER ELEVEN   Fame and Fortune   181

CHAPTER TWELVE   Family Riches   195

CHAPTER THIRTEEN   A Sinner Saved by Grace   211

CHAPTER FOURTEEN   Our Town Built on Life Enrichers   221

CHAPTER FIFTEEN   An American Citizen   233

CHAPTER SIXTEEN   Hope from My Heart   247

CHAPTER SEVENTEEN   Adventures in God's World   261

CHAPTER EIGHTEEN   Promises to Keep   273

ACKNOWLEDGMENTS

I'VE TRIED TO CAPTURE in this book some of the memories and lessons I've learned in my life. I give God the glory for the people I've worked with who have helped me along the way. This includes, first of all, my partner, Jay Van Andel. We were friends since high school and in business together more than fifty years. God's hand was truly on this remarkable relationship.

I also give God the glory for my wife, Helen, to whom I've dedicated this book. As my marriage partner of more than sixty years, she has participated in so many of my memories and lived through so many of my life experiences. It was only natural that Helen played a big role editing this book.

Immeasurable credit goes to all of the many other people who have helped shape my life and the lessons contained in this book as well as those who contributed time and energy to this project. These individuals are too numerous to mention, but you know who you are and I am most grateful to you.

This book would not have been possible without Marc Longstreet and Kim Bruyn. I am the talker, and Marc captured my words and helped me write them down. It was Kim who told me, "You can do it!" when she encouraged me to write "one more" book and who also guided the project from start to finish.

INTRODUCTION

I'VE BEEN A CHEERLEADER most of my life, from leading cheers in high school to cheering on people to seize opportunities and realize their dreams. Cheering others on has taken me to nearly every country in the world. I've met hundreds of thousands of people along the way. I wrote this book for all of them: the millions worldwide who have their own businesses through Amway; the thousands of Amway employees who cover the globe; members of the Orlando Magic organization and Magic fans; the business, government, and community leaders I worked with in my hometown of Grand Rapids, Michigan, and in central Florida, where I now reside; fellow church members; leaders of

Christian, political, and educational causes; many others whose life paths have crossed mine; and those I've yet to meet as I continue to travel around the world. I hope all of them will in some way enjoy and benefit from my life journey and the lessons I've learned along the way.

This book is not a full-blown autobiography containing every detail of my life. Yet it does go into much greater detail than my previous books—including *Believe!, Hope from My Heart,* and *Ten Powerful Phrases for Positive People*—and paints a more complete picture of the experiences that have shaped me, been most meaningful in my memory, and taught me important life lessons. I hope you will enjoy a "behind-the-scenes" look at some of the events of my life, in many of which you may have played a role. I will also be gratified if you pick up a few ideas that might be helpful in your own life.

My previous books all have included my thoughts on the importance of perseverance, faith, family, freedom, an upward look, and other values. I touch on those values in this book, but looking back at eighty-eight years of life, I believe one principle rises above the others. People who achieve the highest levels of success—whether in business or in raising families or simply in discovering fulfillment and satisfaction and purpose in life—are those who place their focus on other people rather than themselves. I have succeeded only by helping others succeed. My friend and partner Jay Van Andel and I discovered that this was at the heart of the Amway business we started and built together. If there is only one lesson to be gained from my life story as presented in this book, I hope it is that viewing each person as a unique individual created by God, with personal talents and a distinct purpose, is the most important thing. That truly has been my key not only to success but also to fulfillment and abundant joy in my life.

PART ONE

ACTION, ATTITUDE, AND ATMOSPHERE

CHAPTER ONE

Growing in the Right Atmosphere

MY GRANDFATHER'S GIFT FOR the art of selling was almost magical to me. I don't know if I was a born salesman, but I remember as a boy being fascinated by my grandfather and other men like him in my neighborhood. Their livelihoods in those hard times depended on their talents for selling.

My grandfather would let me ride with him in his Model T truck as it sputtered and rattled through our streets, filled with the fruits and vegetables he bought from farmers in the morning and then sold door-to-door. He was a people person; housewives who interrupted their cooking and cleaning, wiping their hands on aprons or dish towels as they came out of their houses at the sound of his truck horn, seemed to be attracted as much by his humor, easy demeanor, and conversation as by the color and freshness of his produce.

It was on that route that he gave me my first opportunity to try to make a sale. I earned just a few pennies, but that memorable achievement was a definitive moment in who I became as a man.

I can't dismiss my roots as a kid growing up during the Great Depression in the ordinary midwestern town of Grand Rapids, Michigan. From the standpoint of money and material possessions, we were barely scraping by. But I remember my boyhood years as a happy time of rich experiences. Life was friendly and cozy and easy. Even the need for hard work and sacrifice during those tough times made me stronger and taught me important life lessons. I was fortunate to grow up in the right atmosphere.

My foundation was built at home and the homes of friends, on the streets and playgrounds, in classrooms and church pews; from my parents and grandparents, teachers, and pastors. I learned how to run my own business as a paperboy. I experienced the rewards of that first sale from my grandfather peddling produce door-to-door. I wrote and delivered my first speech as senior class president in high school. My budding Christian faith was planted and nurtured during family devotions and in Sunday school. I was assured by the lasting bond and successful partnership of a loving mother and father. I gained a confidence and optimism from my father's constant encouragement, and first began to think of myself as a potential leader because of the kindness of a wise and thoughtful teacher.

The Grand Rapids where I was born on March 4, 1926, was nothing special as American cities go. Our claim to fame was being called "Furniture City" for the number of companies manufacturing home furnishings. I remember a postcard from my boyhood years: "Welcome to Grand Rapids, Furniture Capital of the World." The banks of the Grand River, which runs through Grand Rapids, were lined with brick furniture factories, their smokestacks printed with each manufacturer's name: Widdicomb, Imperial, American Seating, Baker, and others. In those days, electric streetcars rattled along the downtown main streets of Monroe Avenue and Fulton Street, the cars on the road were of the Model T era, and trains still rumbled across the trestle bridges over the river. Traveling a few miles east from downtown on Fulton Street, you came to my neighborhood: two-story, three-bedroom homes on quiet, treelined streets; a smattering of mom-and-pop retail stores; the nearby forested campus of Aquinas College; and plenty of parks to play in.

My family, like most others in Grand Rapids, was of Dutch descent. I can still hear the thick Dutch accents that were so common in my neighborhood: first-generation immigrants still speaking of family back in the "olt country," pronouncing *j*'s as *y*'s and *s*'s as *z*'s ("Yust put the dishes in the zink"). The Dutch who immigrated first to Holland, Michigan, and then found

3

their way to greater opportunities in the nearby, much larger city of Grand Rapids, were hardworking, thrifty, practical, and strong in their Protestant Christian faith. They were lured to America not so much by economic necessity as by the promise of being free to be able to be whatever they could dream to be. Letters still survive of Dutch immigrants writing home to brag about the freedoms they enjoyed in America, which were unimaginable in the Netherlands of that time—where if you were born a baker's son, for example, you likely would always be a baker.

The Reverend Albertus Van Raalte, who in the mid-1800s founded Holland, Michigan (whose residents still celebrate their Dutch heritage annually by dressing in traditional clothing and wearing wooden shoes during Tulip Time), wrote in a letter to the Netherlands that most of the Dutch seeking work in Grand Rapids were unskilled and lacking in education. Fortunately, many of the men were able to learn to be skilled craftsmen in the furniture factories, and many of the young ladies were maids in rich people's homes. But there were many others who manifested another Dutch trait: having an entrepreneurial spirit. Three of the largest religious publishing houses in the nation were started by people of Dutch heritage in Grand Rapids. The Dutch established in Grand Rapids the headquarters of the Christian Reformed Church and founded Calvin College. The Hekman Biscuit Company started in Grand Rapids and later became the Keebler Company. And you may be familiar with a chain of Midwest superstores called Meijer and an international direct-selling company called Amway, both founded in Grand Rapids by Dutch Americans. So I owe much to my Dutch heritage: a love of freedom, a solid work ethic, an entrepreneurial spirit, and strong faith.

I was born during the Roaring Twenties but have no memory of that volatile era when America was progressing rapidly to a seemingly ever-greater prosperity. My childhood memories are of the era known as the Great Depression. When I was ten years old, President Franklin D. Roosevelt was elected to a second term and in his inaugural address he reminded Americans that he still saw a third of the nation ill-housed, ill-clothed, and ill-fed. A quarter of Americans—at a time when most homes depended on a single breadwinner—were out of work. My father was out of work, having lost his job as an electrician and needing to make ends meet with odd jobs for three years. We could no longer keep the house that he had built and where I'd spent several wonderful years of my boyhood.

My first house was on Helen Street, where I was born at home in the days when most families could not afford deliveries in a hospital. My second home was on Wallinwood Avenue, where I remember that polishing the floors was a satisfying chore because we were so proud to have hardwood instead of plain wood floors. The house had three bedrooms upstairs, and the only bathroom was downstairs, which was typical for houses in my neighborhood in those days.

When my father, Simon, lost his job, I had to move with him and my mother, Ethel, and my younger sister Bernice back to

Helen Street into the upstairs rooms of my grandparents' house, where I remember sleeping under the attic rafters. My father rented out our Wallinwood house for twenty-five dollars a month. While the move was hard on my parents, I remember viewing it as kind of an adventure sleeping in an attic. It was also a fun way to spend more time with my grandparents. While I didn't realize it at the time, that experience gave me perspective and a much greater appreciation in my later years when I achieved a level of success that afforded me and my family a very comfortable lifestyle.

We lived there for about five of the worst years of the Depression. We were poor but no poorer than most of our neighbors. We didn't think it unusual to get our haircuts from a neighbor who had a barber chair in a bedroom of his house. Ten cents was a huge sum in those days. I remember a teenager coming to our door selling magazines and crying because he couldn't go home until he sold the last one. My father had to tell him honestly that we didn't have a dime in the house. But those weren't bad days for me as a boy. I felt safe and secure in our tight community. We lived in a Dutch-American ethnic neighborhood, so I also felt a sense of belonging. I grew up in a community on the eastern edge of the city called "the Brickyard," named for three brick factories that were built next to some clay hills that were mined to make bricks and tiles. The factories employed the hardworking new arrivals from the Netherlands, most of whom did not yet speak English but found a welcoming and familiar community in the Brickyard.

Our community was close not only because of our common Dutch ancestry and because so many extended families lived together, but also because of physical proximity. The houses were tall and skinny, mostly two stories and built very close to each other on small lots separated by very narrow driveways. The houses on narrow streets and alleys were so close together that neighbors could borrow from neighbors without ever leaving their houses. They just stretched a little and passed whatever was borrowed through a window.

In addition to my grandparents, my cousins lived in the neighborhood. I remember growing up with family discussions around the dinner table and plenty of playmates in the backyard. Few grandparents today live with their children and grandchildren, but I have fond memories of the benefits of their love and wisdom. Despite some struggles, I recall much more love than worry. I believe we are more a product of our homes than of any other single influence. Later in life, as a young father of four children, when I traced my development in the home and the influence of my parents, I remember being sobered by the enormity of the responsibility. What seemed so natural and easy as a child takes on a whole different dimension as an adult when you finally grasp all the conscious effort it takes to create a home life with the right atmosphere.

Before today's diversions such as television, computers, and video games, we had to be inventive in making our own fun. Some of the best times I remember were spent inventing activities for my sisters and playmates to enjoy. The younger of my two sisters, Jan, still remembers me as a great fudge maker who created a lot of different types of flavors of fudge. I even rigged up a string system to pass fudge from our kitchen window to a window at our neighbor's house.

I loved sports, but with few resources, I also had to be creative to be able to play. I built my own basketball hoop, and I flooded a vacant lot in the winter to create a frozen pond where we went ice-skating. I remember the echo of Ping-Pong balls off the concrete floor and brick walls of our dark basement, where I taught my sisters to play on a table next to the old coal furnace. Jan still recalls my wicked left-handed spin.

I also have fond memories of playing baseball with my cousins in the street. In hard times, there were fewer cars on the road. Our ball would get so beat up that we'd have to wrap yarn around it and stick rags inside because we couldn't raise enough money in those lean times to buy a new one. Playing ball in the street could be hazardous to neighbors' windows, and we likely broke one or more. I do remember one irate neighbor woman—we must have been intruding on her property too much for her taste. She ran from her house wielding a butcher knife and yelled at us to get off her lawn.

The best part of the day was listening to shows on the radio like *The Green Hornet* and *The Lone Ranger*. On Sunday afternoons our family would work jigsaw puzzles while listening to a mystery program on the radio. When we finished one puzzle, we would swap it for another one from our relatives. I remember walking to a relative's house about two blocks away, carrying five boxes of puzzles and trading them for whatever puzzles they might have. My grandparents had a card table in their home that always was covered with puzzle pieces and a puzzle in progress. Everybody in the house would stop by and put a piece in until the puzzle was eventually finished. I also read books, but because of the expense and lack of new books, I had to settle for whatever was on the bookshelf in our house. These were usually older books, so by default I was reading *Tom Sawyer* and other classic literature. A real treat for me was the penny I got each Saturday, which I usually spent on candy.

As I reflect on the childhood activities that filled my life, I really think in many ways it was a blessing that circumstances forced me to be innovative in creating fun and engaging others in the process. It certainly helped shape my ability to think creatively and come up with new ideas, and it also helped develop my social skills. Kids today—including my own grandchildren—are too focused at times on computers and electronics and not enough on personal interaction.

I grew up even before the age of television, when parents in the evening read their books and newspapers, spent time with their hobbies, or took walks, and children played under the streetlights. Long before the existence of backyard patios and decks, people spent more time on front porches and conversed with neighbors passing by. Before air-conditioning, the sounds of neighbors talking, or their radios, wafted through the windows on the summer breeze. Those were days when you could still hear the clip-clop of horse-drawn wagons on the streets, the chugging of Model T cars, the calls of peddlers, the clinking and clanging of the milk and ice deliveries, and the clatter of coal tumbling down chutes into coal bins.

My parents instilled a strong work ethic early on in my life. One of my chores was to keep our furnace stoked with coal every morning and evening. Our coal deliveries were dumped onto our driveway, so I first had to transport loads of heavy, dusty, and dirty black coal into our basement and then open the creaking cast-iron door and shovel coal onto the glowing embers in the furnace. The work kept us from freezing during those harsh Michigan winters, but our house still remained cold by today's standards of forced-air furnaces. My sister Bernice still remembers that house being so cold that we had to stand over a furnace register while getting ready for school. For heat we had coal, and for refrigeration we had ice. Neighbors would post signs in their windows with the number of pounds of ice they wanted delivered. I once joined a friend on his ice-delivery route and remember lugging fifty- and hundred-pound blocks of ice up stairs and wedging them into people's iceboxes after making room by rearranging their milk and food. Each icebox had a drip tray for the melting ice, and I recall many a time when I'd pitch in with my sisters to mop up a flooded kitchen floor because we forgot to empty the tray.

With my parents as role models, I accepted work as part of life and essential to a successful home and family. My sister Bernice may have remembered later in life hating to dust the rungs on all the dining room chairs, but I don't recall her ever as a young girl complaining or refusing to do simply what was expected of her as a contributing member of our family.

In our Dutch-American community, Sundays mostly meant going to church and Sunday school. Going to church was not optional. We were part of the Calvinist, Dutch Reformed tradition. We lived by a clear set of rules: honor your parents, set aside money for the Lord's work, give to others, be honest, work hard, and strive for good mental attitudes. We did not share a meal before first giving thanks for it in prayer, and when the meal was over we'd read a portion of scripture.

Nearly every business closed on Sundays. Alcohol was frowned upon, and dancing and even going to movies were suspect or considered by some of our church members a waste of time. The two main denominations in our community were the Reformed Church in America, introduced by Dutch immigrants in colonial times, and the Christian Reformed Church, which separated from the Reformed Church in America for reasons that few members still recall. Our family attended the Protestant Reformed Church, which broke away from the Christian Reformed Church, and is the strictest and most traditional branch of the three. Members typically attended both the Sunday morning and evening services in our big redbrick church.

I've known the feel of the wooden church pew from my earliest recollection. For a young, rambunctious boy who enjoyed being active in sports and playing outside with friends, sitting on hard church pews and trying to grasp a pastor's rather lengthy prayers and solemn sermons was not always easy. By the time I was old enough to ride to church with a friend in his car, we would occasionally grab a bulletin from the back of the church and leave without attending the service—later showing the bulletin to our parents as proof that we had been in church that morning.

While I did not become a professing member of the church until after I was an adult, I eventually came to appreciate why faith and church membership are important and taken seriously in our Dutch culture. Even as a boy, I never doubted that one's faith matters. I cannot remember a time when I did not believe in God. By the time I was in high school I saw a difference between people who were Christians and those who were not. I just sensed a general atmosphere among Christians—greater warmth, a surer sense of purpose and meaning, and a deeper bond among those who share a faith. I made up my mind that the Christian group was where I belonged.

Even as we enjoyed fun and games as kids, we could not escape the fact that we were living through tough times and that my father was out of work. He was taking whatever work he could find to keep the family going. During the week he sacked flour in a grocer's back room, and on Saturdays he sold socks and underwear in a men's store. But he never complained. My father was a very positive man. He believed in the power of positive thinking, and he preached it even though his own life wasn't as successful as he would have hoped. He read the same authors I talk about today—Norman Vincent Peale and Dale Carnegie. He only had an eighth-grade education, but he was interested in learning through those positive-thinking books. He would always tell me, "You're going to do great things. You're going to do better than I've ever done. You're going to go farther than I've ever gone. You're going to see things I've never seen."

Looking back, I think my father probably felt a lot of stress during the tough economic times of my childhood, even though he didn't let it show. When I reflect on his amazing example of leading our family with such a positive and optimistic attitude, I hope in my younger years I somehow expressed my admiration and appreciation to him. Even more so, I hope I've been a similar example to my children. We shouldn't try to live through our children and grandchildren, but to this day I try hard to play a role in helping my children and grandchildren fulfill their potential for successful, meaningful lives. I can truly now appreciate how my father wanted the same for me.

Having lost his job, my father encouraged me to go into business for myself. His experience was that he had no control over being employed or unemployed. His destiny was in the hands of his employer. More important, he convinced me that being a business owner was not an impossible dream. He always taught me to believe in the unlimited potential of individual drive and effort. Any time I'd say, "I can't," he'd stop me and say, "There's no such word as *can't*." He impressed on me that "I can't" is a self-defeating statement. "I can" is a statement of confidence and power. My father always reminded me, "You can do it!" Those words stuck with me and guided me for the rest of my life.

Likely because I was the oldest child and only son, my father showered me with attention, playing sports with me, reading to me, and sharing his hobbies. He influenced me in so many areas that later would have a tremendous impact on my life. He liked to "putter," as we said in those days. I remember watching him in the basement, tinkering with anything mechanical that he could fix. He was also a visionary and an adventurer, a lover of new ideas and dreamer of places he would like to see. Because of the expense of travel, he could not go to the places he only saw on maps, but I do remember our family once piling into our only car for a road trip to Yellowstone National Park, which was a big adventure for us.

Dad was also ahead of his time in his interest in nutrition. He talked about organic gardening before most people even knew what that was, preached the benefits of a healthy diet, and allowed only whole-wheat bread at our table, which my sisters hated. His unique opinions and practices in the area of nutrition no doubt influenced my receptiveness to later becoming a Nutrilite distributor with my future business partner, Jay Van Andel.

I also was fortunate that my mother was a good influence on my life. She did not work outside the home and could always be there for my sisters and me. Unlike my father, my mother admitted that she was not very positive during those years. Yet she was a stabilizing force, ensuring a well-kept home and meals on the table, with a practicality and thrift that got us through those lean years. She was a warm, loving lady who was supportive and helpful. She taught me how to make fudge. She helped instill my work ethic, insisting that each child do household chores. You had to set or clear the table or do dishes. I usually ended up having to dry the dishes as my mother washed them, and it was our routine that allowed us to spend time together each evening and chat—something I think is often lacking in today's culture.

She also was clever in making the most of the little we had. For example, every year she would rearrange the furniture; because we couldn't afford new furniture, rearranging the furniture at least gave a different look to the living room and the appearance of something new. She also was instrumental in my education about money. She gave me my first "penny bank" to save coins I earned doing odd jobs around the neighborhood. I dropped as much as I could spare into that cast-iron bank, and once a month my mother would walk with me to the bank to make a deposit into my own savings account.

Needing to earn money during these hard times, I started delivering newspapers—which essentially was my first business, when I think about it. Delivering the *Grand Rapids Press* taught me responsibility, accountability, and all the principles of the rewards of hard work. Every day a bundle of papers was dropped near my house for the area paperboys. I counted the number of papers needed for my route and sat along the street with the other paperboys, folding paper and sticking them into the big cloth bag that I strapped across my shoulder. I had thirty to forty customers and learned to serve them well. I walked my route for several months, but I quickly set a goal to save enough money to buy a used bike, a black Schwinn racer, to make my job easier and the delivery process more efficient. I still remember the thrill of buying that bike as a result of a goal I set and the money I earned and saved—another valuable lesson I've carried with me my entire life about the rewards of work. I also perfected throwing papers from my bike so they hit the porch, and occasionally getting off my bike and retrieving any that missed and landed in the bushes. My excellent service paid off each Christmas when many of my customers would give me an extra twenty-five or fifty cents or, on rare occasions, even a dollar.

Every Saturday morning I had to go to each house and collect their subscription money. After each customer paid me I'd punch the little card they hung on a nail by their door. This first business venture taught me all the basics—I learned that I had to go out and get business, how to take good care of my customers, and how to collect money and make change.

The job also gave me a new sense of freedom and mobility—not to mention the means to earn a little money. I delivered papers to some of the nicer homes in my area, but I never felt I was a "have-not" in the world of "haves" and never resented or was jealous of these customers. I could see they lived better than my family, but instead of envying them I remember having the attitude that what they had, I, one day, could get. I believed that by working hard I could get where they were someday.

The other key introduction to the world of business was through one of my grandfathers, who gave me the thrill of my first sale. Both my grandfathers lived in our neighborhood, and both were businessmen.

My grandpa DeVos owned a little store that sold groceries, a few dry goods, and household items and clothing that he ordered for customers from a catalog. He also sold penny candy from a big counter at the front of the store. The store was right across from a school playground, and I remember the schoolkids coming in to buy candy from my grandfather, carefully scanning the array of colorful choices behind the glass before deciding how to get the most for their one or two pennies.

He also lived above the store, so if customers came in when he was having lunch or occupied elsewhere, he would hear the doorbell ring. If he was praying before a meal and a customer came in, he would stop midsentence and yell, "Yust a minute!" finish his prayer, and then go downstairs to wait on the customer. He also drove a horse and buggy through the neighborhoods, taking and delivering orders.

My mother's father, Grandpa Dekker, was an old-fashioned "huckster," a term that comes from an old Dutch word meaning "to peddle." He drove his Model T truck to the public market each morning and bought vegetables that he then sold door-to-door to customers along his neighborhood route. He arrived at each home, rang a bell or honked the horn or called out, "Potatoes, tomatoes, onions, carrots . . . ," and the housewives would come out of their homes to buy his produce.

That batch of onions left over after my grandfather finished his route was my first sale, but it was just the beginning. After that, whenever my grandfather had leftover vegetables, I sold them. It took salesmanship and persistence, but I loved it. Those experiences and lessons from my paper route and household chores were the foundation for becoming, at a young age, a diligent worker with a sense of responsibility, an eye toward detail, and an appreciation for pleasing customers. When I was just fourteen, I got a job at a neighborhood gas station. In those days, drivers relied on their small, nearby gas stations, typically owned by a neighbor with mechanical skills. Most of these gas stations had two pumps out front and a single stall for tuning up and repairing cars. Many attendants wore uniforms, with caps like those worn by police officers and their shirt collars fastened with bow ties. In addition to pumping gas, washing the windshield, and checking the oil and water, these stations provided other car-care services, and I got a taste of them all.

I worked all day on Saturdays just washing cars. This was before the days of car washes and heated garages, so customers relied on their gas station to wash their cars in the winter. Washes cost a dollar, and my cut for each car was fifty cents—so even in winter, I bundled up each Saturday morning and washed as many cars as possible. Many roads were unpaved, and cars had a lot of dirt around the windows and door frames. I wiped everything clean and built a reputation for thorough car washing. Using what I learned from my father, I also helped the mechanic find car parts and do simple repairs like replacing generators.

I became so dependable that the owner put me in charge of running the station when he had to be out of town—even though I couldn't have been more than fourteen years old. That was a real confidence booster, to know that people trusted me at that level. I learned at a young age what it meant to be responsible for a business, another important lesson that would serve me well in life.

I also was still a teenager when I got an after-school job as a salesman in a men's clothing store. I was really doing an adult's work, but I liked the opportunity to deal with customers in a more professional setting, and I discovered I also was pretty good at sales. I would have rather played sports after school like many of my friends, but I needed money to pay my parents for room and board and because each family member was expected to help put bread on the table.

Our high school baseball coach once said to me, "I see you're a lefty. Would you like to play ball?"

I said, "I'd like to, but I can't. I go to work every day after school, so I can't practice."

———

LIFE TOOK A QUICK turn on an unusually warm Sunday afternoon in early December 1941. I was peddling my Schwinn bicycle when a neighbor boy called to me from down the street, "Did you hear the news?"

I said, "What news?"

And he said, "We're at war! The Japanese have bombed Pearl Harbor!"

That's how I found out about the war on December 7. Of course, from then on we all listened to our radios and picked up from the newspaper what was going on in the war. That was always the news of the day. Lowell Thomas became famous as a reporter for his fifteen-minute news broadcast every evening on the radio and his narration of movie theater newsreels. I'll never forget his distinctive, melodic voice, which gave each story an added air of urgency and excitement and a sense of romance about faraway places that many Americans had never heard of before the war. World War II created new shortages in addition to all we had been sacrificing because of the Depression. No cars were manufactured after the 1941 models came out. Materials ranging from paper and rubber to metal and food were in short supply because so much was needed for the war effort. We planted Victory Gardens so farm crops could go to the war effort and used ration stamps for groceries and gasoline. People did a lot of canning of the fruits and vegetables they grew in their gardens. I remember helping my mother and the glass jars of tomatoes, pickles, and other canned goods that lined the wooden shelves in our fruit cellar. The war first really hit home in our neighborhood when a doctor who lived near us lost a son who had gone overseas to fight as a Marine gunner.

I was starting high school, which was another turning point involving lessons of hard work, accountability, and sound decisions. When I was a fifteen-year-old freshman, my parents sent me to a small Christian high school in our city. Like most teenagers, I never appreciated that a private school costs money and that my parents had to sacrifice to pay my tuition. I just goofed off, flirted with girls, and paid little attention to homework and grades. Somehow I managed not to flunk any classes that first year. My Latin teacher gave me a barely passing grade—just to keep me from taking her class over again! At the end of the academic year, my father said, "If you're just going to fool around, I'm not going to pay all that extra money to keep you in a private school. You can goof off in a public school, and it won't cost me anything."

So the following year he sent me to Davis Tech to learn to be an electrician. At this trade school I was labeled as "not college bound." I was miserable that whole year. It was a wake-up call about all I'd lost by goofing off in school. I told my dad that I wanted to go back to the Christian high school.

He said, "Who will pay for it?"

And I said, "I will."

I found odd jobs to earn the money, and the second time around at Grand Rapids Christian High School I was a better student. I learned that you appreciate what you earn much more than what is given you. I also learned that decisions have consequences. My decision to goof off in school had negative consequences, and my decision to return to Christian High had positive consequences that followed me the rest of my life.

Grand Rapids Christian High also was where I began to learn and develop leadership skills that would enhance my success in business. Even though work prevented me from playing sports, I found another outlet. Our school had no organized cheerleading squad at basketball games, so I decided to lead cheers. I just stood courtside and started yelling cheers and doing cartwheels the length of the basketball court to stir up the crowd. At that point I was starting to wear apparel from my job at the clothing store and I remember doing some of my cheers in a suit and tie. My antics must have really put a strain on the seams of my clothes, because one time, in front of the whole student body, I did a cartwheel and ripped the seat of my pants. I walked red-faced and backward off the court. But I didn't let that embarrassment stop me.

I loved getting the crowds and the team fired up. Cheerleading has carried over to the rest of my life. I still refer to myself as a "cheerleader" because I keep encouraging others to have confidence and to use their talents to follow their dreams. It's been one of the most important reasons for my success and my helping others succeed.

Unfortunately, I had less success in the classroom than on the gym floor. Getting up and motivating people, making friends, and socializing suited my personality much more than sitting in class. While my grades were better, they were still somewhat marginal, and I had no goals. Somewhere in the back of my mind was a fuzzy notion of one day being a business owner, but I had no clear idea of when and how that might happen. I don't remember how my name got on the ballot, but for some reason I was in contention for senior class president. I had been away at Davis Tech for a year and thought I'd been forgotten, but maybe my fame as a cheerleader and ability to make friends boosted my popularity. Even some of my teachers were pulling for me to win. One day our teacher left the classroom for a few minutes, returned, and said to me, "You won! I was so excited and hoping you would win that I had to leave and go find out."

As class president, I was expected to speak at our commencement ceremony. America had just survived the Great Depression and was fighting against the Nazis and Japanese in World War II to protect and preserve our American way of life. I eventually would go on to speak to crowds of thousands about the greatness of America—its opportunities superior to any other country in the world. Even at this young age, I was filled with hope and optimism. I focused my commencement speech on the strength of our country and the optimistic outlook for its future.

I titled my speech "What Does the Future Hold for the Class of 1944?" My father helped me rehearse in front of a mirror, coaching me on diction, gestures, where to pause, and which words to emphasize. I dedicated myself to delivering a speech that I hoped would inspire my classmates who, along with me, were commencing new lives. Many would be joining the fight for freedom in Europe and the South Pacific. I delivered the speech at the Coldbrook Christian Reformed Church in downtown Grand Rapids. I don't recall being nervous, but I remember thinking my delivery was good and recall the crowd applauding. After the speech, a mother in the audience even told me, "You were a lot better than the preacher." This was high praise in our Christian community, where the only oratory most people experienced was a Sunday sermon.

One more experience in high school would forever change my life and the way I saw myself. When I graduated, my gentle, scholarly Bible teacher, Dr. Leonard Greenway, wrote a line in my yearbook that I never forgot—just one simple line of encouragement: "To a clean-cut young man with talents for leadership in God's kingdom." His line was simple but a great source of inspiration to a young man who was not a good student and had been told he was not college material. But a teacher whom I admired had seen me as a leader! Wow! I'd never thought of myself in that way before.

Years later I met Dr. Greenway again at a high school reunion. I was emceeing the event, and I sort of put him on the spot by asking him in front of my classmates if he remembered what he had written in my yearbook. He stood up and repeated the line perfectly after all those years. I was impressed. He recognized something in me that he must have sensed I had not yet seen in myself. He was wise enough to understand the power of a positive line of encouragement in helping shape a young person's future. To this day I remember his kindness, and in tribute to him and what he did for me, I continue to try to encourage others with the power of positive phrases.

So, I was blessed to grow up in the right atmosphere. I had the love and encouragement of a close family, the positive attitude of my father, and the selling and business examples of my grandfathers. I inherited the best traits of the Dutch: their faith, thrift, practical lifestyle, work ethic, and appreciation of freedom and opportunity. I honed my talents for speaking and leadership as senior class president. My faith was nurtured and strengthened in my church and at Christian High. I learned the value and rewards of work as a paperboy and from the odd jobs I did to pay my school tuition. Even in the depths of the Great

Depression, I was surrounded by people of persistence and hope. I was encouraged by supportive teachers. And I was a cheerleader, an optimistic and enthusiastic role I continue to play today.

After I became known as a motivational speaker, one of my key speeches was "The Three A's: Action, Attitude, and Atmosphere." Too many people fail to act because they are frozen by fear and doubt. But nothing happens until we act. Our actions stem from a positive attitude. And a positive attitude is developed when we are in, or choose to put ourselves in, the right atmosphere. My atmosphere was the love of my close-knit family and community, which, through strong faith and hard work, found happiness despite the Great Depression and held on tightly to hope for a better tomorrow. Whether with my own children, my NBA Orlando Magic players, or millions of Amway distributors worldwide, I continue to emphasize the necessity of the right atmosphere. If you are surrounded by friends who are negative, leave and find positive friends. Stay away from places and situations with potential for negative behavior and incidents. If a negative atmosphere pervades where you live or work, go elsewhere. Seek out friends, business associates, and mentors with positive attitudes who share your goals and best interests.

A positive atmosphere nurtures a positive attitude, which is required to take positive action. Because of my atmosphere, I had a tailwind while still a high school student and was confident of one day achieving my stated goals. But as influential and important as all my childhood experiences were in shaping my future, nothing would be as significant as one person I would meet before I graduated from high school, and who would be instrumental in changing my life in ways I never could have dreamed. And it all started with a simple ride to school.

CHAPTER TWO

Starting a Lifelong Partnership

THE STREETCAR RUMBLED TO a stop at the end of my street. I was attending a Christian school that was two miles from my house, and occasionally the streetcar conductor would see me, wool coat collar up, hat pulled down, and black galoshes sinking in the snow, and give me a free lift to school. He must have noticed that I was walking much farther to school than most students, and knew that the walk likely felt even longer facing into the wind and falling snow. I sometimes took a city bus, but the route wound through downtown Grand Rapids and made several stops before arriving at Grand Rapids Christian High School. Allowing the extra time for the long bus ride to school meant rising long before the sun.

I needed more efficient transportation, and already being an enterprising type, I had an idea. I had noticed a 1929 Model A Ford convertible with a rumble seat going by several times on East Fulton Street near my home. I started noticing the same car in the parking lot at my high school. I thought a ride in this car would surely beat the bus, the streetcar, or walking. So one day at school I introduced myself to my fellow student who was the car's owner. I told him I lived just a couple of blocks from him and asked if I might be able to catch rides with him to school. He was an enterprising type as well and said to me, "Why don't you give me twenty-five cents a week to help pay for gas?" Gas was about ten cents a gallon in those days, so I agreed to the deal, not yet realizing that he already was charging other students twenty-five cents a week for rides.

That was my first formal business arrangement with Jay Van Andel, who became my lifelong friend and business partner.

Jay's father, James, and another Dutchman, John Flikkema, owned the Van Andel & Flikkema auto dealership, which is still in business today, and which was why Jay had the unusual privilege as a teenager during the Great Depression of driving his own car. When I first met Jay he was a studious, quiet guy. He was also an only child, and compared with my home, it struck me he lived in a quiet house with parents who were rather reserved. I was outgoing and not a serious student. Jay was reserved and a serious student who seemed to me to be able to get straight A's in school without cracking a book. So I was first attracted to him not because we had anything in common but only for his car. He had a couple of friends that he had gone to church with and who lived on his edge of town before he moved out to the east end on Fulton Street, where I lived, but he had few friends in his new neighborhood.

We started our relationship as strangers who were unlike each other not only in personality but also physically. I was shorter and stockier with dark hair. Jay was tall and slighter with wavy blond hair. I was outgoing; he was shy. I could make people laugh; Jay had a dry wit that more often evoked smiles. He was a junior in high school when I was just a freshman. He didn't say much, wasn't much for small talk, but he was interesting because he was curious about subjects beyond what was typical for kids in high school. I may not have had the patience to be a scholar, but I liked expanding my horizons, so we gradually got to know each other and were able to carry on interesting conversations.

I eventually asked him during a ride to school, "Why don't you go to the ball game tonight?" I don't know if he even realized I was talking about a high school basketball game or if he'd ever been to one of our games, but he said, "Yeah, I bet it'd be fun, okay." So we went to the basketball game together. We started regularly going out to basketball games, and of course meeting other friends at the games and going somewhere afterward for Cokes and burgers. So, as my new friend, Jay was exposed to a little different mix of people and made some friends at school. We started doing things together, socializing together and double dating.

Many years later, an article in *Reader's Digest* referred to Jay and me as the "Dutch Twins." That was untrue in several ways, because of our different looks and personalities, yet true in that we were so much alike in our worldview and philosophy. Looking back, I see a level of maturity in our friendship, especially when so many people never get to know one another because they are too quick to judge people on how they might look and because their personalities don't match one's own. Jay and I were an unlikely pair, but had we never made the attempt to befriend someone who outwardly might appear to be different from ourselves or acted different from ourselves, we never would have discovered how much we thought alike.

Before long, Jay not only was making more friends, he was using his knack for enterprise to find more paying passengers. His Model A car would occasionally be loaded with our school buddies, overflowing into the rumble seat and even standing outside the car on the running boards as they held on for dear life. This was long before seat belts and today's safety standards, but Jay didn't exceed the city's twenty-five-mile-per-hour speed limit, so the police left us alone, maybe thinking this was the best transportation that kids during the Depression could afford.

I had a basketball hoop at home, and I can still see Jay in his little car, pulling up, not joining the game but hanging around while we shot baskets. He would come in my house with us, and my mother would feed us. My mother liked Jay a lot—but what mother wouldn't like her son hanging out with a more mature, enterprising, studious type who drove a car from his father's auto dealership? Our relationship just deepened as it went along. I brought him a little life and activity, and I learned a lot from him because he was so smart.

It turned out to be a pretty good mix.

Jay's father also got to know me well enough to offer Jay and me our first opportunity to work as partners and test our ability to succeed with adult responsibilities. I was only fourteen and Jay sixteen, but Jay's dad must have trusted us and seen a reliability and capability beyond our years. He asked us if we would be interested in driving two of his pickup trucks from Grand Rapids to a customer in the faraway town of Bozeman, Montana. Would we ever! Auto production during the war was limited to vehicles for military use, so owners of large farms in Montana were buying pickup trucks wherever they could find them. Asking and trusting two kids with that responsibility is unimaginable today. But boys were expected to grow fast in the days when so many young men were overseas fighting in World War II. The need for boys to do men's work during the war also made it possible for me to have a driver's license at age fourteen.

My mother said to Jay's dad, "Jim, he's not old enough to go driving across the country like that."

"They'll be just fine," said Jay's dad. "They're big boys."

So with my mother's lukewarm blessing, just as a boy today hops on his bike to ride around the block, I was going to hop behind the wheel of a pickup to drive more than a thousand miles to

Montana. Planning the trip was all Jay and I could talk about, and I doubt that in our excitement we got much sleep the night before hitting the open road. We most likely lay awake with visions in our heads of the Wild West, mountains, prairies, and ranches. Money was tight and hotels were few, so we slept on hay piled in our truck beds. We had a tow bar so we could ride together in one of the trucks and tow the other. There were places we stopped where we knew people. In Iowa there were a few people from the Christian Reformed Church and other kids older than us who were going to Calvin College in Grand Rapids. We made a few stops at these homes, and our hosts would feed us royally. One of these families, likely of German descent, served sauerkraut—I remember the family laughing so loud when they saw the look of disgust on my face as I tasted it for the first time. I hated it.

Before the age of freeways, speed limits tended to be around forty miles per hour, and roads were two lanes and laid out along county lines. So we would drive for miles, make a hard left turn at an intersection, drive in that direction for a while, and then turn right, and repeat that several times over. That's the way the roads went, because the priority was the farm, not the road. We drove through Iowa and then through South Dakota, where I remember stopping at the famous Wall Drug Store in Rapid City, and then through the Badlands, where we came upon an icon familiar only from our schoolbooks: Mount Rushmore.

Our truck tires were nearly bald when we left Grand Rapids. I remember having three flats on the same hot day. We fixed the tires with a patch kit we had brought along. A service station in the middle of nowhere wanted to charge us a nickel for air. Even an extra nickel was beyond our travel budget, so we ended up working up a sweat in the sun as we inflated the tires with a hand pump—another early lesson in thrift and self-reliance.

This trip revealed the sense of adventure that was ingrained in both our business and personal lives. The journey also gave us a firsthand look at America and an appreciation of our country, which would one day help define our principles and style of business. We also received lessons in teamwork, self-reliance, responsibility, building trust, and the satisfaction in a job well done. We have always enjoyed travel. Our Nutrilite business in later years, for example, required trips to the company headquarters in California a couple of times a year. We liked driving back and forth to California, always stopping to see national parks and to ski in the mountains. Through our rides to school, having fun after school, and being alone together on the open road for an adventure that would be the dream of any teenager, our friendship was cemented. By the time I graduated from high school, we knew each other like brothers and were expert judges of each other's character. We were convinced we were friends for life. During my senior year of high school, Jay wrote in my year book: "True gold never corrodes."

I miss those days when very young men could experience such adventures. I think today there's a tendency of many parents, likely out of fear and worry, to play it too safe with their children. These "helicopter parents" hover over their children and try to pick them up whenever they stumble. We do a disservice to our children when we don't let them fall a few times before they learn to walk on their own. In today's more complex and less safe world, allowing a fourteen-year-old to make the same driving trip Jay and I made to Montana is no longer possible, but I appreciate my parents trusting me and giving me an adventure of a lifetime. That trip was important in helping Jay and I start growing from boys into men. And I'm sure now that both my dad and Jay's dad knew that would be the case.

I don't recall many specifics about what we talked about on those rides to high school. I'm sure we discussed our mutual desires to one day go into business for ourselves, but like most boys of our age we likely talked more about sports, girls, or a tough test coming up in school. But I do remember that most of what we talked about was the war. It's hard to imagine now, but in those days small talk took a backseat to the overwhelming topic of World War II. Everything was secondary to what was happening in Europe and the Pacific. Those faraway conflicts reached across the oceans to touch everything in our lives. We picked up our newspaper off the porch, and the bold headline across the front page was about a battle won or lost. Black-and-white photos showed our soldiers marching across Europe and Marines hitting beaches. Every radio broadcast included the latest war news in lands with unusual names and the meaning of winning or losing each battle. Movietone News in theaters showed helmeted German soldiers and their tanks rolling across Europe. Jay was deeply interested in the logistics and stories of the war, had opinions, and liked to discuss what was happening in Europe and the

South Pacific—places so distant and exotic to two boys from Grand Rapids. For these two boys who would one day found a company based on America's unique freedoms and free enterprise system, I believe we even held a special interest in our country's struggle for freedom against the dictatorships of Germany and Japan. Every boy who sat in a movie theater on a Saturday morning and saw the newsreels of Hitler, Mussolini, and Tojo strutting before manic crowds of thousands knew the high stakes of the Allies defeating these enemies. They also were eager to join the fight and help win the war.

By the time Jay graduated from high school in the spring of 1942, talk about the war and watching the war unfold in newsreels was replaced by the reality of war. Jay joined the Army Reserve Air Corps that fall as a private and later received his commission as a second lieutenant, training crews for B-17 bombers. When Jay left for active duty, he left his Model A car behind for me to keep driving to school. Those were happy years of friends, fun, and achievement, but in the back of my mind I realized that once I turned eighteen, I, like so many young men my age, would be enlisting to serve my country in one of its greatest challenges. I graduated from high school in June 1944 and joined the Army in early July—student to soldier in a matter of weeks.

Everyone who joined the military in those days was thinking the same thing as what was going through my mind: "We gotta win. I want to serve." Men rejected for service because of a health problem were very sad. If you were 4F, everybody knew it. So you were happy when you passed the physical, knowing that you could go in and serve. Maybe that's hard to believe today, since the controversy of the Vietnam War and the elimination of the draft. Since that time, only those who choose to serve fight our wars. I would never wish for any young American to have to fight in a war, but I believe we have lost a valuable bit of our American patriotism and spirit of willingness to sacrifice for country that was so alive and vital when we all knew our future as a free country depended on winning a world war.

Jay became a bomb-sight officer, teaching people how to maintain, repair, and realign bomb sights and how to run bomb drops. On a bomb run, the bomb officer takes over the airplane. The pilot sets the plane on its course, but once over the bomb site the control transfers to the bomb officer. So Jay became expert in maintenance of the bomb sights and the training of people to run them. Soon he was sent to Yale for officer training, and he became an officer very quickly thereafter. He was smart enough to learn that stuff. In one of Jay's many letters to me while we both were serving, he wrote from a base in South Dakota that it was his birthday and that he was in his office, in charge of the air base as the officer of the day. It was a Sunday and his turn to be in charge. He was still just twenty-one and in charge of all these bombers, soldiers, and airmen. Only in times of war can we trust people so young with so much responsibility.

I had hoped to become a pilot when I enlisted. By the summer of 1944, the war was beginning to wind down, and the Air Force decided that no more pilots needed to be trained. Instead, they assigned me to be a mechanic for gliders that would be used to drop troops and equipment into combat. My service began at the train station in Grand Rapids, wearing civilian clothes I'd soon be giving up for a drab green military uniform, and with a government-paid ticket to Chicago in my pocket. I remember waiting on the platform with my parents, who were struggling not to show too much emotion but also worried about their only son being in harm's way far from home.

Later in my service I remember traveling all over the country in trains packed with troops and the natural camaraderie and boisterous behavior during those trips. Because I was naturally outgoing, I actually thought it fun to jostle shoulder to shoulder in packed train cars with soldiers eager to help win the war. But on this train ride—my first of any great distance, whose destination was a very large city—I was alone with my thoughts. I listened to the rattle of the rails and gazed out the window at the midwestern farms, small towns, and factories between my hometown and the second-largest city in America. I had a lot to ponder during those few hours on the train.

Like everyone in my situation, I thought about the real possibility of the dangers of combat and losing my life. Every day the newspaper printed names of servicemen—including some names familiar to me or even young men I knew—who were seriously injured or even had sacrificed their lives in the war. I understood my life was at stake, that I might be going into dangerous areas, and that I might not be coming home. My thoughts then—and later, during the war—turned to a more serious contemplation of my faith. Faith takes on huge meaning in the military because of the preciousness of life, the awareness of people dying, buddies of yours alive one day and dead the next. Life and death were present and in front of me all the time. So religion becomes more serious, and you decide what you believe and what you don't.

The war strengthened my faith, and I drew comfort from the fact that the Lord was watching over me and guiding my life.

Yet I was proud that I had volunteered, and I shared the country's dedication to winning. We could not imagine the alternative of a dictator taking over our country and having to do what Herr Hitler told us to do. That thought of the dictators, swastikas, and parades of goose-stepping soldiers that we saw in newsreels was frightening for Americans. I was determined to do my part to help save my country. And I was later able to not let the thought of dying hang over me. The possibility of death is always a part of war, but those who are very young always think it will happen to the other guy. Times were tense, but rather than dwell on the danger or even talk about it, we just did what was ours to do. I also was struck on that train ride to Chicago with the thought that I was leaving home and might not return for many months.

I later learned that for men serving overseas in the military, one of the most profound words that touch their hearts and minds is *home*. Home takes on a new, wonderful meaning as a life value. Many who served in the war wanted to see the world and were glad to get away from the house, but they later were glad to have a house to go home to.

My connection to home was the letters I received from my

parents, family, and friends who kept me updated on the daily activities on the home front. My parents and I exchanged letters at least once a week. The troops looked forward to mail call, because even if people back home were writing regularly, that didn't mean receiving regular mail. Getting mail to troops was challenging, because friends and family didn't always know where their loved ones in the service were stationed. They only knew they had to write to the post office in the Pacific or the Atlantic.

Jay and I also kept up our correspondence, and he wrote the letters that meant the most to me, especially when I was thousands of miles from our hometown on a tiny island in the Pacific. I wrote him some rather mundane updates about my daily service, but Jay's letters to me were more detailed and philosophical. He wrote about a lot of stuff because he thought about a lot of stuff. His letters made me feel at home and reminded me of the depth of our growing friendship.

Like me, Jay was nostalgic for home. He once wrote: "I feel awfully lonesome tonight, Rich. I guess it's the weather, these cool days toward the end of summer. There's something in them that makes me think of autumn back home. How wonderful it would be if you and I and the whole gang were home again this fall." In another he wrote specifically about our friendship: "Our two lives are linked so inseparably, two pals who click in such perfect unison, a friendship so firmly sealed, shall not be parted by a war. We shall continue where we left off, and fulfill all our dreams, with the countless addition that two friends in perfect accord will make. Your best friend and pal as always, Jay." These letters are still some of the best reminders I have of our special friendship.

Too often we speak casually about "friends." Anyone today who is an acquaintance is called a friend, so closer relationships have to be called "close personal friends" or "best friend forever." People today even have thousands of "friends" on Facebook. In our day, a friend was a friend, and it was a rare and special relationship.

So I had my government train ticket to Chicago and orders for where I was to report once I arrived. The train station in Chicago was bustling with men in uniform and military bands playing. From Chicago I boarded a train for Sheppard Field, a major recruit-training center on the Texas-Oklahoma border, where I was one of 7,700 aviation mechanics trainees. I was assigned to maintain gliders, which would be dropped from planes to carry troops and supplies behind enemy lines—silently.

After a year and a half training in the States, I received my orders in the spring of 1945 to travel to a base on the tiny Pacific Ocean island of Tinian, southeast of Japan. By the time I got my orders, the Germans had surrendered, and the war with Japan appeared to be drawing to a close. I was traveling by car to Salt Lake City on August 15, 1945, when I first heard news on the car radio about the war ending in the Pacific. The radio signal was fading as we traveled higher in the mountains, and we were unable to find a station anywhere on the dial. As we dropped into the valley, the signal returned, and we had confirmation that the Japanese had surrendered and the war had indeed finally ended. I celebrated in Salt Lake City along with everyone across the country. Guys in my unit were especially excited because we thought that we probably would no longer have to go overseas.

Despite the war's end, they shipped us overseas anyway. I spent six months on Tinian, which was the island from which the *Enola Gay* bomber flew to Japan to drop the first atomic bomb on Hiroshima. I helped dismantle an airfield that our troops had built after capturing the island from the Japanese. I drove a little truck on a speck of an island in the Pacific. My job was not sophisticated, but I knew the work was still important and I was proud to play a role.

Jay was disappointed that he never got overseas. As he later explained to me, his unit was in New York boarding a ship for Europe. Suddenly they stopped the line of boarding troops. An officer shouted, "We can't take any more; we're full. All of you from here on back need to report to your barracks." Jay later said, "By the time they got to the V's, the ship was full. I couldn't go—all because I was a Van Andel instead of a DeVos."

The war exposed me to men of different faiths and backgrounds, from across the United States to the South Pacific. My service taught lessons about discipline, doing what you are told to do, and keeping yourself physically strong—and also a lot of things about command, the rigidity of the military, and awareness of how you must have clearly defined rules and directions when you have a huge number of people. I did as I was told, never realizing at the time that one day my partner and I would need some of the same principles to manage an international business with thousands of employees and millions of distributors.

My service ended in August 1946, when we sailed from Japan to San Francisco, and I took a train to Chicago. I was twenty years old, matured by my wartime experience and life far from home. I was eager to join a confident, victorious nation in economic progress and becoming a light of freedom for the world. Everybody was excited, and it was the most confident period I've lived in. We had proven our ability to work together to overcome adversity and achieve greatness. We were ready to get back to work and buy new cars, home appliances, houses, and all that had been in short supply during the war years. We were optimistic about making a good living and doing better than ever before. Military guys coming home were opening gas stations, stores, and other businesses or grabbing jobs and working hard. We had won a war in which that terrible guy Hitler was trying to kill us and take over our country and Japan was eyeing other parts of the world for its expanded empire.

Now America was free to reach for the stars.

When we arrived home after the war, Jay and I were no different from other veterans who were eager to seize opportunity in this new America of seemingly limitless promise. We had already even planted the seeds of a business plan during the war. Jay was once home on leave before I had left to serve, and after returning home from a double date one night, Jay and I started talking. I asked him, "When the war is over, what are you going to do? Go back to college?" But given our backgrounds and desire to fulfill our dreams as business owners, I think we both knew college would not be an answer for either of us. The more we talked, the more we realized we should form a partnership and start our own business.

Lifelong partnerships in business are rare. The reasons for our lifelong partnership and friendship seemed so simple and natural but are hard to put into words for anyone who has not experienced such a unique relationship. The beginning was so inconsequential: a deal of twenty-five cents a week for rides to school. Just a few years later in a time of war, Jay is writing me as "your best friend and pal as always." We are in my parents' garage, barely men, proposing the formation of a business partnership.

I've spoken to audiences in my later years about the power of partnership. Very rare is the lone businessman who has all the wisdom, knowledge, skills, and talents to make it on his own. Jay and I knew that from the start. I believe he was drawn to me because I introduced him to a world of social activity, the joy of making and keeping friends, and embracing the enjoyment and wonders of life with the enthusiasm of a cheerleader. And I came to respect Jay's wisdom. Even in high school he always dealt with a worldview. He was well-read and smart as could be, remembering everything he read. Just in ordinary conversation I learned a lot of things from Jay that a kid his age should probably not have known. His dad was in business, so he also had a little business knowledge. He worked on cars at his father's auto dealership on Saturdays, which gave him both a work ethic and some mechanical skills.

Jay and I first worked together when we would tinker with his Model A at his father's business. I liked Jay because he was a smart guy, and he must have liked me because I dragged him away from his books to go out and have fun. During our school days, he would be home reading a book. I would ask him, "Jay, you wanna go to the game tonight?"

He'd look up from his book and answer, "Well, I haven't thought about it."

I would say, "Come on, let's go."

"Well," he would say after pausing from his reading, "okay, if you're going to go, I'll go with you."

We say that opposites attract—or the whole can be greater than the sum of its parts—or whatever. Jay and I were two different parts that somehow meshed to make everything work. I needed a ride to school. He had a car and moved into my neighborhood. God opens doors. Had I not walked through that door, my life likely would have turned out to be very different. When I'm asked if I could have succeeded as I have without Jay, my answer is simple: "Nope." And I'm sure Jay would have answered in the same way. Shortly before his death in 2004, Jay told his younger son, David, "The number one thing you must do is protect the partnership."

I wrote a birthday note to Jay after we had been together for more than a quarter century, which he saved for the rest of his life. Maybe the sentiments in the note sum up our rare friendship and partnership better than my attempt at an explanation:

"Happy Birthday! Just a note to tell you how much you have

meant to me personally. Over the past 25 years we have had our differences, but something greater has always shone through. I don't know if there is any simple way to say it, but it could be called mutual respect. A better word could be 'love.' The years have been good to us in so many ways that it is difficult to isolate specifics, but the thrills and joys are mainly in the fact that we have done it together. It really did begin with that 25-cents-a-week ride, and it's been one beautiful ride ever since. Love ya, Rich."

By the end of World War II, Jay and I had no question that we were best friends and potentially successful business partners; we were confident in each other's abilities, knew we complemented each other, and, above all, we trusted one another. I, in fact, trusted Jay with my life savings from my military service as my investment in our first business together. We would start a rather unique and risky enterprise, but we both were confident that it would take off.

CHAPTER THREE

Try or Cry

WHEN I WAS JUST twenty, I bought an airplane. I didn't even own a car yet. I was still in the Army Air Corps with no clear idea of how I was going to make a living once Uncle Sam sent me home in a few months. Call it youth, or inexperience, or simply the overwhelming optimism in a victorious America at the end of World War II, but I sent Jay all the savings from my government paychecks to invest in the purchase of an airplane— at a time when few Americans had ever flown in a plane, let alone owned one. Like many young men in the early era of flight who were enamored of daring pilots like Charles Lindbergh and the exploits of fighter and bomber pilots in the war, Jay and I both liked airplanes. We were convinced that planes would become as popular as cars in postwar America. We'd been working around airplanes and gliders as members of the Army Air Corps, and planes were constantly taking off and landing on air bases where we were stationed. The United States had built millions of planes, from single-pilot fighters to huge B-17 bombers, to defeat the Germans and the Japanese in air battles over Europe and the Pacific. The thought was not too far-fetched among many Americans that houses would be built near airstrips and there would be an airplane in every garage.

With the rising popularity of air travel, Jay and I saw a potential demand for a business built around airplanes. So why not pool our savings and buy one? I was still overseas but trusted Jay's judgment. I asked my father to give Jay my savings of seven hundred dollars as my share of the down payment on a plane. My military pay was sixty dollars a month and I had sent most of my money home for my parents to save for me. My dad knew Jay and Jay's father. He trusted Jay as much as he trusted me, so he just gave Jay the money and never questioned my decision.

Jay bought a two-seat, propeller-driven Piper Cub plane that he found in Detroit. Not knowing the first thing about flying, he hired a pilot to fly our new plane to Grand Rapids. To earn money to pay off the Piper Cub, we opened Wolverine Air Service, which we named for our home state of Michigan.

We had a third partner, Jim Bosscher, a friend of ours from high school and a wartime airplane mechanic, but soon after starting our business, he told Jay and me that he was more interested in a different career path. He decided to go to Calvin College, then went on to receive his Ph.D. in aerospace engineering from Purdue and became a professor at Calvin. His life goes to show that we all have different gifts, which lead us to succeed in different ways. He did not become a business owner, but he went on to receive a doctorate in engineering and lived a fulfilling and rewarding life.

Millions of men were coming home after the war with hopes and dreams, filled with confidence and ambition and a desire to start careers, open businesses, or complete a college degree. To help them, the federal government enacted the GI Bill, which offered veterans funding for job training and higher education. The GI Bill could be applied to pilot training, so we were in business. Most men returning from the war had little idea of what they were going to do next, so I was happy with my investment of seven hundred dollars to be in a new business.

Wolverine Air Service likely first came to the attention of people in Grand Rapids through an early promotion. Jay put our new plane on display in a car showroom on a busy corner in the heart of Grand Rapids and held an open house. Hard to believe today, but back then many people had yet to see an airplane close up and were curious enough to stop by and take a look at our exotic winged vehicle. Sales and promotion would actually become our end of the business. Neither of us knew how to fly, so we

hired a World War II P-38 pilot and a B-29 pilot as our flight instructors, along with an Army Air Corps airplane mechanic. This
freed Jay and me to focus on promoting the service and finding
students.

We printed handbills for our approved flying courses, tout-
ing, "Learn to Fly. If you can drive a car—you can fly a plane."
We appealed to potential customers with our pitch that airplanes
were the future and that training for veterans was funded by the
GI Bill. Our training would be a good way to get in on the
ground floor for careers as pilots or in the aviation business. To
excite them about the offer and seal the deal, we also offered
them a free airplane ride and let them experience as much as possible the feel of flying. Selling flying lessons was just a matter of
building relationships with people who came to the airport to see
what flying was all about. We captured the imaginations of potential customers who gazed down at their hometown from a
mile up in our floating aircraft and who dreamed of actually
being pilots one day.

The Piper Cub plane was not sophisticated, nor was our operation in the early days. The airfield in Comstock Park, a few
miles north of Grand Rapids, was still under construction.
When I say a field—that's basically all there was to the airport at
that time. The owners were running out of money to complete
construction, so there were no hangars and they had stopped
building the runway. Jay and I had to improvise. We put pon-
toon floats on our plane and took off and landed on the Grand
River, which ran along the airfield. Jay recalled our first office as

a tool shed, but I distinctly remember dragging a chicken coop down to the river, cleaning it up and whitewashing it, and slapping a sign on the door—and that became our first base of operations.

The airport was eventually completed, but in the meantime, Jay and I constructed our own building at the site for a second business that was unrelated to aviation. We put up a twenty-four-by-twenty-four-foot wooden prefabricated building—we'd found a kit at a home show that included instructions and all the parts. We unpacked all the parts, followed the directions, nailed the pieces together, installed the electrical wiring, and ended up with the building that would house our next new business: the Riverside Drive Inn. Because our planes had to be grounded before dark, our jobs ended each day just before sunset. Rather than waste our evening hours, we thought opening a restaurant would be a way to make some extra money from people who worked at the airport, kept planes there, or simply drove there to watch airplanes. Jay and I had remembered seeing several "drive-in" restaurants on an earlier trip to California and thought we could transfer that innovation to our home state. With an investment of three hundred dollars we opened on May 20, 1947, one of the first drive-in restaurants in Michigan.

I realize some people may find it hard to believe that two young guys could have accomplished so much. Today we expect young people to finish college first and get some experience working for others before they start businesses of their own. But I think it was simply the times we lived in—and the fact that very early in life we were expected to work and were given responsibility. I can't really explain it myself. All I know is that Jay and I had a lot more energy about everything than doubts about anything. Those were the days when Americans were still known for "Yankee ingenuity," backyard mechanics, and do-it-yourselfers. We "tinkered" more before our era of sophistication and specialization. On occasion I'll read about people today who start successful ventures in their early twenties, and I applaud them and am thrilled that this tradition continues. I encourage all young people to get a college education but would never discourage a young person with a talent and a dream to just go for it if they feel they have everything they need to succeed.

We had no experience in running a flying service, but we actually knew more about airplanes than about running a restaurant. My kitchen experience was limited to eating my mother's cooking and drying the dishes. A small drive-in, fortunately, is not a sophisticated business, and we kept things simple. Our little white clapboard building, with the RIVERSIDE DRIVE INN sign on top of the shingled roof, was only big enough for our old gas stove, a counter, a refrigerator for drinks, and a freezer. We had no tables for indoor dining and served all our food on trays that we delivered outside to cars.

The airport location was still new and remote, so at first we had neither electricity nor running water. We bought a gasoline-powered generator that rattled on the floor and made a racket we barely could hear over. Besides the constant roar and gasoline fumes, the generator gave us just enough electricity for the lights. We had to power our stove with bottled propane. We hauled water to the restaurant in jugs we filled from a well a few miles away. We kept our menu simple—hamburgers that we fried in butter in cast-iron skillets, hot dogs, and the bottles of soft drinks and milk from our refrigerator.

Jay and I would take turns flipping burgers and delivering orders to the customers' cars. About the biggest mistake we could make was overcooking burgers and having to throw them out. I think we each remember the other doing so at least once. In our parking lot Jay and I put in four-by-four-inch posts that we wired with lights. Each post had a clipboard on a nail with menus attached. Customers would press the light switch when they were ready to order, and either Jay or I would run out to their car to take their order. Hard to imagine today these two flight-service owners in aprons sweating over a gas stove of burgers sizzling in butter and running back and forth between their kitchen and the customers' cars. To promote our air service, we had a photo taken of us in our office— two young executives in matching flight jackets looking important as we consulted over a chart. That scene was far removed from our night jobs, hustling and sweating as carhops and burger flippers.

The Good Lord blessed us with a lot of energy and ambition. Even though we were running two full-time businesses from dawn to past dark, we also were looking for new opportunities. For a while we rented canoes on the Grand River next to the airport. We bought an ice-cream vending business from a man who had about a dozen pushcarts he wanted to sell. We bought his carts and hired students during the summer to peddle Fudgsicles and paddle pops to kids in the neighborhoods. We also arranged with charter boat owners to offer fishing excursions on Lake Superior.

Even after long days, Jay and I still had the energy to go to a hamburger joint in Grand Rapids to talk business over a burger swimming in butter. Or we would go to my parents' house or his—my mother would feed us one night, and his mother would feed us the next night. Neither of us had the outlook or inclination to be idle. On cloudy or rainy days, when our planes couldn't fly, we found ways to be productive instead of using the weather as an excuse not to stay busy. In fact, we vowed that one day we would start a business that did not depend on the weather, daylight, or when people ate dinner.

With twelve airplanes and fifteen pilots, Wolverine Air Service eventually became one of the largest flying services in the state of Michigan. During the course of our business, Jay and I took our own advice and both earned our pilot licenses. In those days, completing ground school and flying hours took little time to be qualified to fly these small, two- or four-seat, single-engine propeller planes. Years later, I also completed the training to be licensed to pilot twin-engine planes. Controlling a plane and buzzing over the familiar landmarks of my hometown, over the Grand River, or along the shores of Lake Michigan, was a thrill that has never left me.

For me, flying and owning planes became a lifelong interest. As the Amway business grew, we bought our first plane, a Piper Aztec—and when our business extended to the West Coast, an impractical trip for the Aztec, we turned our thinking to the purchase of a jet. Happily, we had hired a business consultant early on who, when we began to think of buying it, said, "I don't care what you spend your money on. If it'll keep you out on the road talking to distributors and speaking at meetings, buy it." So we did. And when that one was always booked, we bought another . . . and another . . . and finally built our own corporate hangar to house the fleet.

I maintain that without computers and without airplanes our business would not be where it is. We believe in personal contact; if we didn't have planes, we couldn't get out there to make it happen.

Wolverine Air Service was an amazing training ground for Jay and me. We learned by taking chances and doing, and moving ahead confidently—as we would for the rest of our lives— even though at times we should have looked before we leaped. In our early days as pilots, for example, we were running low on fuel and landed our seaplane on a small lake in Northern Michigan. The people in that area were not used to seeing a plane on their lake, so many approached in their boats, and we felt like celebrities. We managed to find some gasoline to buy but discovered that the lake was too small to allow us enough distance to build up the speed required for takeoff. We ended up tying the plane's tail to a tree, and while one of our pilots revved the engine, Jay cut the rope, and the revving plane shot forward and lifted off the water to just barely clear the treetops on the other shore.

Experience really is the best teacher, and we learned a lot from our first real business. We learned how to promote and to sell a service to customers. We learned management and bookkeeping. We had our first experience with government, because we had to keep records of our services in order to justify our funding from the GI Bill. Jay had to drive to Detroit with the invoices for all the flying we'd done and the lessons we'd given and all the other documentation required. The routine was quite involved in order to get a check from the government. We developed our first commercial banking relationship with Union Bank in Grand Rapids. But when the GI Bill ended, so did our source of revenue and our business.

We probably cleared $100,000 over the four years in the aviation business, and we likely broke even on the restaurant. The flying service wasn't a big moneymaker—not the kind of return you might expect for the effort we put into it. But we were young, just getting started in life, and were quite satisfied with the results. Two young men with no business experience starting a successful air service seems pretty remarkable, in hindsight. But we almost took it for granted, because we had known even before the war ended that we wanted to achieve something of significance. A letter from Jay to me during the war best sums up our feelings at the time. He wrote: "Look, this is not our final chapter. This is only a step along the way.

This war will end at some point and we will go back to our lives, and at that point we have to make the decision of what it is that we're going to be doing with our lives and be remembered for." I recall it was only a question of what kind of business we were going to get in, not a question of whether we were going to get a job.

During these early years of our partnership, Jay and I were sharing a small cottage on Brower Lake, on 10 Mile Road, about ten miles north of Grand Rapids. We also owned a 1940 Plymouth car together that we bought from his father. Our little cottage was only about five hundred square feet, about a quarter of the size of a typical home today. But it was still big enough for a kitchen, a bar, and a little dinette and a door that led to a bathroom with a bedroom on either side. Jay and I slept on bunk beds in one of the bedrooms. I somehow got the lower bunk, maybe because Jay was taller than me. Because we were still in our early twenties, our little cottage became a natural hangout for other young men who had recently returned from the war, as well as their wives or girlfriends.

I also had one of the first TV sets in town—a box about two feet high with a screen that was no more than eight inches across, and a rabbit-ear antenna. Friends from our high school and military days were drawn to our cottage to experience television, have parties, and maybe swim in Brower Lake or ride in the little outboard speedboat that Jay and I bought with our business earnings. Jay was often content to stay home and read, but he was willing to go with me, at my urging, to a movie or a get-together with friends. Jay was not a natural party lover, but once he arrived, he was fine with socializing, even if at times he might have preferred to be home. Jay was much more interested than I was in dreaming about adventure by reading books. But it was a book that sparked both our imaginations and led to our next adventure.

In the winter of 1948 we both read *Caribbean Cruise,* which describes the sailing experiences of a fellow by the name of Richard Bertram. He was a boatbuilder who, with his wife, sailed a forty-foot boat to the Caribbean and around its many islands. The book was the story of their trip. We were fascinated by this yachtsman's exploits and his descriptions of the white beaches, palm trees, and blue waters of the Caribbean. We both had been working hard with little time off and thought a sailing trip would be relaxing, not to mention an adventure even more exciting than our road trip to Montana as teenagers. We planned to sell our businesses and thought we would have both the money and time to enjoy ourselves. We believed the trip would be fun and decided we had to go.

After paging through a yachting magazine and finding a sailboat broker in New York, we flew to meet with him and start looking for boats. He took us to several shipyards until we finally found a boat that met our needs and that was within our price range. The boat, *Elizabeth,* was resting in a boat cradle on an asphalt parking lot in Norwalk, Connecticut. She was a thirty-eight-foot, two-masted schooner with a long bowsprit and three portholes in the cabin, which had plenty of room below for our small crew of two. She appeared to be a sound boat—and as many people said a pretty little boat—but *Elizabeth* had been in dry dock for all the years of the war. She had been sitting on her keel without the bow or the stern being supported, so her two ends sagged a bit. Her wooden hull also had dried out, which we would soon discover causes the wooden slats to separate and let in water. However, marine surveyors told us *Elizabeth* was fit, and other boats were hard to find right after the war, so we sold one of our planes and bought the boat.

The condition of our new boat was one potential hazard. The other was that Jay and I had never had our hands on the tiller of anything more sophisticated than our little outboard and a small sailboat on Brower Lake. Sailing a thirty-eight-foot boat on the ocean is not for amateurs. So, while Jay returned to Michigan to close out the airplane business, I hired a captain and a crew member to teach me sailing while we sailed south to Wilmington, North Carolina.

With the captain asleep one night, I made a navigational error and landed in a New Jersey swamp. An amazed Coast Guard sailor said, "I've never seen a boat this far inland before." I went home at Christmas and returned with Jay to our boat in North Carolina, where we set sail on January 17, 1949, for Miami. Once there we planned to outfit our boat for the Caribbean and sail at least as far as Puerto Rico. Leaving the dock, I yelled to Jay, "Throw out the bowline!" He threw out the bowline, and I was going to get the stern line, but I was a little slow getting to the back of the boat. As I was trying to release the stern line I realized that the tide had changed. When we had docked the tide had been fine for landing that way, but when we tried to go away the next day, the tide was running in a totally different direction. Our boat turned around so the bow was where the stern had been. I heard a loud bang and saw that our hull had struck our little aluminum dinghy, which was tied up behind. The impact dented the dinghy, and that dent was a souvenir of our first sailing mishap.

Usually when you put a dry wooden boat in the water you let it sit in straps, and within a day or so the wood will have absorbed enough water to tighten and seal the seams. Well, *Elizabeth* never tightened up, even during our long trip from North Carolina to Florida. Our boat didn't have a float on its pump that lifts with the rising water to automatically trip the switch that starts the pump, so we had to remember to check the water level in the bilge and flip a switch on the pump as needed to remove any standing water. If I didn't get out of bed at 3 A.M. and flip the switch, I would be walking in water when I got up at five or six. After six hours or so, the water would rise above the floorboards. We accepted this routine as a way of life. It was a pretty little boat, after all, but we kept waiting and waiting for it to tighten up. Once we got to Florida we had the boat hauled out of the water and everything tightened up and recaulked. We also had all the crabs, clams, barnacles, seaweed, and everything else that sticks to the bottom of a boat in the ocean scraped off to keep *Elizabeth* sailing as fast as possible.

I wish I could say the rest of our trip was a pleasure cruise and great adventure. The truth is, our voyage did not live up to the romantic cruise that Bertram described in his book, which had so intrigued Jay and me. We actually worked our tails off and had some miserable days on the high seas. Traveling long distances in the ocean in a boat as inefficient as ours was hard work. Heading into the wind meant tacking back and forth rather than traveling in a straight line. We would work hard all day zigzagging 150 miles to make 50 miles of forward progress. With changing tides and different ports, every docking situation was unique. With our lack of experience, I spent most days worrying about docking and most nights worrying about getting away from the dock. I'm on record for encouraging people to follow their dreams instead of worrying about not having enough experience, or fearing failure, but looking back at this sailing trip, I have to admit we could have been better prepared.

We had a lot of close calls that could have been disasters but weren't only because somebody with more experience bailed us out. One day we were trying to land at a fuel dock where boats were nose to the shore right in front of us. As I approached the dock, I went to put the boat in reverse, and the engine quit. So now our boat was moving along pretty good, heading right for the side of a docked boat. As I said earlier, *Elizabeth* had a pretty good-sized bowsprit jutting from her front. Jay threw a line to a guy on the fuel dock. He grabbed the line, threw it around a piling, and ran. Fortunately we had the bumpers out on the side of the boat and the line really stretched but didn't break, and gradually it stopped the boat from plowing into a dock or another boat. We were lucky to avert what could have been a serious accident.

On the way from Miami to Key West, the fitting in the aft deck that holds the mainsail in place pulled out of the wooden deck, leaving us little control over this sail. Residue that had been left in the gas tanks since before the war contaminated the gasoline, which in turn fouled the engine carburetor. We were heading into the harbor at Key West at dawn when the engine quit. We also were unable to use the sail that had pulled out of the deck. So, our boat was rocking and slapping the water, the loose main sail was flapping, the engine was dead, and we were trying to drop anchor right in the channel. Suddenly we heard a horn blaring and saw a big submarine approaching from the Key West training base. The submarine did us no harm, but we later were cited for anchoring in a passageway, even though we had little choice.

But the biggest challenge was the leaking. Not only did the hull leak, but so did the planks over our cabin. The leaking deck dripped cold water onto us. We had to find ways to plug the leaks, catch the water in buckets, or drape something over our heads. We had an inadequate heating system, and water in the Atlantic Ocean can be cold on foggy and cloudy winter days.

From Key West we sailed to Havana, Cuba, which in those days was still a great tourist town. The streets were bright at night from the lights of casinos, bars, nightclubs, and hotels. The Cubans made rum for the drinks that were popular in Havana. Cruise ships from Miami brought American tourists to the Cuban capital, so the streets were crawling with Americans shopping by day and hitting the bars and casinos by night. Quite an awakening for two kids from the small midwestern city of Grand Rapids!

Leaving Havana, we set sail east along the remaining six hundred miles of the northern Cuban coast, on a course for Puerto Rico. We had sailed probably three hundred miles by March 27, 1949, when we conceded the obvious. At sunset I turned on the electric pump to get rid of about a foot of water in the bilge. When I checked again an hour later, the water level was a foot higher. I said to Jay, "It's deeper. We're not getting rid of it." So we got out a big hand pump and started working to try to lower the water level. But it didn't matter what we did; the water kept rising. Our boat was taking on water faster than we could keep it out with both our electric and hand pumps. With water rising up to our knees, and exhausted from pumping, we finally accepted the inevitable and shot off a red flare. If no boats were in the area, we thought we might be able to make shore in our two-man aluminum dinghy powered by a small outboard engine.

All these years later, I still wonder why we kept sailing so far in a leaking boat. We must have just been young, inexperienced, and in denial. Even when we thought we might sink in fifteen hundred feet of water about ten miles offshore, I remember us staying calm. I still don't have a good answer for this feeling of calm that has stayed with me throughout my entire life. I guess I have been blessed with the assurance that whatever storms life may bring my way I will endure. That has been a prevailing truth through the ups and downs of each new venture in my life.

Fortunately we were in a major shipping lane, and the *Adabelle Lykes*, a freighter headed for Puerto Rico, answered our distress signal at 2:30 A.M. She showed up not a minute too soon, as a plank in our bow broke loose and water started pouring in. She pulled alongside the *Elizabeth*, and the captain shouted down to us.

"Who are you and what are you doing?" For all he knew, we could have been Cuban pirates.

I called back, "We're the *Elizabeth* registered out of Connecticut, and we're sinking."

Once he realized we were just American kids, he threw a rope ladder over the side of his ship and climbed down to our boat. He offered to try to hoist our boat with a crane onto his deck, but our vessel was too weighted down with water. *Elizabeth* was now just a hazard in a shipping lane. So all his crew could do was punch a hole in her side and then use the weight and speed of the freighter to ram her and break her up so she would sink. In the darkness of early morning, Jay and I stood on the deck of the freighter and watched the sailboat that had once been our vessel to adventure slowly disappear beneath the waves. Members of the Lykes family were on board the freighter, and they offered to give us a ride to Puerto Rico and even put us up in one of their staterooms as guests of honor—guests with a fascinating story of an ill-fated sailing adventure and their rescue at sea.

We thought we'd write a letter to our parents to let them know what happened, not realizing that the Coast Guard had been alerted to our rescue and filed a report that already had been picked up by our hometown newspaper. The *Grand Rapids Press* called my father, looking for more information or a response, but he knew no more than the reporter. Our parents knew only that we had been rescued; they had no other details. They were worried and wondering why we hadn't called. We wrote our letter, but it arrived days after the article in the *Grand Rapids Press*. Years later, as a parent myself, I thought, "My poor mom and dad!" They must have been worried sick. I remember how concerned I was when one of our kids was out after curfew, with a car at his disposal. Here Jay and I were on the high seas in an old sailboat, with little experience as sailors. At the time, I think Jay and I considered ourselves as accomplished, responsible young men prepared for any challenge. But I now realize that to our parents, we were also still just their boys.

Our boat had sunk, but Jay and I wanted to continue our original dream of eventually traveling to South America. In Puerto Rico we boarded the British tramp tanker *Teakwood*, bound for Caracas, Venezuela. The captain was not allowed to take on passengers, so he offered us a shilling each to be crewmen. When the ship landed in Curaçao, we decided instead to fly to Venezuela and disembarked. The immigration officials wouldn't allow crewmen to leave ships, because they would often try to immigrate there illegally. The Caribbean island of Curaçao is a Dutch territory, so Jay tried to explain to the officials in their native Dutch. This made matters worse because they were sure no one from the United States spoke Dutch and that we must be communist spies. It also was hard for them to fathom that two guys in their midtwenties were bumming around the world.

The official said, "How do you think you're going to get out of here? I don't want you stuck in our country and having the government bail you out."

I said, "We've got plenty of money." And we showed him the thousands of dollars in our money belts. After holding our passports and checking with American authorities for a few days, he let us go, and we bought our tickets to Venezuela. The exchange rate there made prices too high, so we next flew to Barranquilla, Colombia. We had little idea where we were going on this trip. We'd just look at a map, drop a finger down, and see where it landed.

Barranquilla is at the mouth of the Magdalena River, which flows deep into the interior of Colombia. We boarded an old stern-wheeler that had been transported from the Mississippi for use on the Magdalena—a boat from the days of Mark Twain, with a big paddle wheel on the back, a barge-type deck, and rooms above. On the foredeck was a small herd of cattle that were slaughtered as needed to feed the passengers. Colombia in 1949 was in the middle of a bloody conflict, and there was lots of anti-American sentiment. We saw YANKEE GO HOME signs, and people had an obvious dislike for us and kept their distance because we were Americans. This forced us to learn some Spanish, because no one would speak English to us. We had translation books that we used for ordering food, asking for directions, and getting whatever else we needed by speaking Spanish. Jay and I relaxed on deck chairs in the warm sunshine and took in the sights of the lush green jungle as the boat wound lazily around the bends in the river. The jungle at night was also home to bandits who boarded riverboats to rob passengers, so Colombian troops would stand guard on the riverbanks.

When the Magdalena River became too shallow to navigate, we disembarked. We took a train to Medellín, a plane to Cali, and then boarded a narrow-gauge train for Buenaventura. The toylike train had open-sided passenger cars. After going through a tunnel, Jay and I were covered with soot from exhaust of the locomotive's smokestack that had been trapped inside. We next boarded a combination freight boat and passenger liner for stops in Ecuador, Peru, and Chile, as the boat offloaded bananas and picked up sugarcane and cotton. Santiago, Chile, with its Mediterranean-like climate and friendly people, was so wonderful that we decided to spend a few weeks there and relax after our months of traveling.

Refreshed from our stay, we were able to keep going and ended our South American adventure by traveling on to Argentina, Uruguay, Brazil, and the Guyanas, and then flying back to the Caribbean for stops in Trinidad, Antigua, Haiti, and the Dominican Republic. As much as Jay and I found some of these foreign lands exotic and charming, I also recall a feeling that stayed with me the rest of my life—these countries simply lacked much of the modern development, luxuries, and conveniences that we in America too often take for granted. This is not a criticism of other countries, but simply a reminder that we Americans need to appreciate our own country.

I remember that even as we were watching our boat go down right underneath us, I was thinking, "What are we going to do next?" I didn't think I was going to die, even though I could have. But the experience of taking on and overcoming challenges instilled in me a wonderful sense of confidence. I learned that when you're in trouble, you simply figure out how to get out of it. We also learned that you don't turn back. Just because our boat sank didn't mean we ended the voyage, we only changed the means of transportation. You take what's available and get on your way. In the same way, we were not fazed when that airport runway was not completed and we used pontoons to take off and land on the river. Lack of electricity in our restaurant was not a problem: we bought a generator. Being inexperienced sailors didn't stop us from a sailing adventure to the Caribbean: we learned by doing.

I used these experiences years later in my speech "Try or Cry." The lesson is simple. You can make excuses about not having the right education or experience, not coming from the right background, being afraid to attempt something new or a challenge that appears too daunting. You can sit around and cry about what you perceive as a life stacked against you, or you can try. Just try, and if you fail, try again. In my experience, trying always beats crying. Because we believed in trying, Jay and I experienced in the Caribbean and South America an adventure that could only be a dream for our friends back home. And we kept trying. Our next venture was not conventional. It was even perhaps a bit peculiar to most other people, and it was years ahead of its time. But we said, "Why not? Let's try it."

CHAPTER FOUR

People Helping People to Help Themselves

AFTER TRAINS, PLANES, AUTOMOBILES, and riverboats criss-crossing nearly every country in South America, Jay and I were exhausted yet exhilarated as we sat in the tropical breezes at Copacabana Beach in Rio de Janeiro, Brazil. Our boat sunk, our savings dwindling, and with no prospects for future income, we assessed our situation: no college education, career training, or substantial holdings to invest in a business. But we had succeeded as business owners and agreed that a nine-to-five job working for someone else would not be in our future.

We wanted to continue doing things on our own.

We had no specific business in mind, but we still agreed to continue as business partners. The beach at Copacabana was where we decided to form a business we called Ja-Ri Corporation, a contraction of our two first names, Jay's first likely because he was older. (We would later found another company that would be named for the contraction of two words.) Our feeling was that we had to start something; the only question was what our next venture was going to be. We had talked a lot about some type of new business during our trip, and our travels had set the stage for what we thought might be a profitable business.

Our focus having been on international countries, we had a notion that we might be successful as importers. We brought home a supply of handmade mahogany household items from Haiti that we hoped to sell to merchants in Grand Rapids. We managed to sell a few of these products to store owners, but found stiff competition in retail sales, especially given our inexperience in this sort of business. Our import business was barely a living, but those mahogany housewares generated the first profits for Ja-Ri.

We needed to start some other types of businesses if we actually were going to earn a decent living. We went from one wood product to another with even worse results. Although it may have seemed like a good idea at the time, in retrospect I don't know why we ever imagined that we could be successful with a company making wooden toys. Our Grand Rapids Toy Company began with the manufacture and distribution of wooden rocking horses on wheels for which we were granted a patent. What kid wouldn't want a high-quality wooden rocking horse? The kids might have liked them, but parents apparently weren't ready to pay the price. The business was a disaster. Our biggest problem was that just as we started making our wooden variety, another company started making plastic-molded rocking horses that were much cheaper to manufacture and could be sold at a much more affordable price. For years we had an inventory of springs, wooden wheels, and other parts left over from that failed enterprise.

We did have one venture that was both a moneymaker and a lot of fun. Jay and I were amazed by how many people were interested in our sailing trip once we arrived home. We had taken home movies on our adventure, so we edited the film footage into a travelogue. We developed a lecture to go along with our film and gave presentations in auditoriums to various civic groups in Grand Rapids. Our share was a dollar for each ticket sold, and some of our travelogues drew as many as five hundred people. Besides the income, we were honing our presentation skills to what to us in those days were huge audiences.

I would love to be able to have those movies today and watch Jay and me as very young men crewing our sailboat and traveling through South America. But nobody knows the whereabouts of our films. They either were misplaced or stored for safekeeping someplace where no one today remembers.

Little did Jay and I know when we were scrambling to make ends meet that the product for our future success was right under our noses—already being used by Jay's parents. Decades before today's emphasis on vitamins and minerals and proper nutrition, his parents in the late 1940s were taking a dietary supplement from a California company called Nutrilite. The product was sold not in stores but by independent distributors. Jay's second cousin Neil Maaskant was a NUTRILITE product distributor and sold his products to Jay's parents, who raved about them to us. Jay's parents urged him to invite his second cousin to meet us and explain the NUTRILITE product and business as a possible career opportunity. We both were skeptical and even laughed at the idea of being vitamin salesmen. But in kindness to a relative, Jay invited Neil to come up from Chicago to Grand Rapids on the night of August, 29, 1949, and make his pitch.

I said, "Jay, he's your relative. You listen to him. I have a date."

When I returned from my date that night, Jay said, "You know, it sounds pretty good!" As he was telling me about NU-TRILITE products, he said, "By the way, I signed us up." By the time Jay talked halfway through the night, I agreed it was a worthwhile effort to get going on and drop everything else. So I wrote a check for forty-nine dollars and bought two boxes of the product and a sales kit with some literature to pass out. Just like that, we were in the business.

Once I heard the details, the opportunity appealed to me because the start-up cost for a new business was so small—just forty-nine dollars for the kit containing two boxes of the nutritional supplements, called DOUBLE X, plus literature about how to sell NUTRILITE supplements and build a business. The appeal was that we not only would make our money on a commission of our sales volume, but also could sponsor other distributors into the business and get an override on what they sold. I liked meeting people, and had a proven talent for sales from our flying lesson days, so the opportunity sounded like a natural fit to me. Our check to Nutrilite made Ja-Ri Corporation an official distributorship.

We started talking to everyone we knew—friends, family, neighbors, acquaintances—about the value of NUTRILITE DOUBLE X supplements, which we both started using daily. Eager as we were to do big things in our new business, our enterprise started slowly—and then got worse. We invited a bunch of friends over to our cottage, showed a short film describing the product, and enthusiastically expressed to the gathering how excited we were about this wonderful opportunity. People started heading for the door. One guy stayed behind to sign up but quit soon after. Then things slowed down. Weeks went by without our recruiting a new distributor. We sold a few boxes of DOUBLE X to friends and family who probably were just trying to help us get started in our new business.

With the distance of many years, I can see that this was a defining time for Jay and me. We had begun a new business, with a new product in a new field and with a new marketing plan. Joining Nutrilite tested everything we had experienced, challenged our resolve, and exposed our character. Why in the world did we jump into such an unconventional and untested venture? What gave us the energy and confidence to approach potential customers with such an unknown product? Why did we seem to be unfazed by potential rejection and even laughter? I can only ask why, because I don't have the answers. I realize the fear of rejection is a deal breaker for most people who consider a career in sales. I know many people are crushed by ridicule or laughter. I'm sure Jay and I were not immune. But for reasons I cannot explain, we simply took rejection and any negativity in stride and kept going. Perhaps experience had ingrained this positive attitude within us. Whatever it was, we simply had the capacity or personalities to do whatever it took to brush off objections and just keep going. And I think we also had the distinct advantage of being able to encourage each other through the setbacks.

We were facing some pretty tough headwinds. First of all, while parents urged their children to clean their plates, eat their vegetables, and have a well-rounded diet, almost nobody in those days was taking a daily supplement or talking about nutrition. The Nutrilite sales plan also was new and perhaps suspect. A salesperson receiving a percentage of the sale was business as usual, but the idea of a salesperson receiving a percentage of another's sales was new and may have been a bit baffling in those days. And Jay and I had a third problem. We were still spreading ourselves thin by trying to run and find different businesses instead of just focusing on Nutrilite.

We finally got focused after Neil invited us to attend a Nutrilite convention in Chicago. During the four-hour drive we agreed that if lightning didn't strike in Chicago, it probably never would, and we'd quit our fledgling Nutrilite business. In Chicago we saw a convention of 150 people, the majority in business attire, which gave the gathering the look of a professional sales organization. We talked to people who had quit good jobs to sell NUTRILITE products and others who were just starting but whose enthusiasm inspired us. Speakers touted their success and shared their selling strategies. I started feeling the same as when I was a boy ingrained with my father's positive message of "You can do it!"

On the drive back to Grand Rapids during the last weeks of 1949, Jay and I decided to forget any other ventures and focus exclusively on Nutrilite. If Neil could make a thousand dollars a month in this business, so could we. That was a lofty goal when a hundred dollars a week was considered a good paycheck, but we were now confident and determined to make it happen. We were so excited, in fact, that on the way home from Chicago we stopped for gas and sold a box of NUTRILITE supplements to the station attendant. Our biggest obstacle was still the fact that the NUTRILITE products preceded today's acceptance of the benefits of vitamin supplements, and the multilevel marketing plan was a new concept. We were a bit like vegans trying to convert customers at a hamburger stand.

Nutrilite was started by Dr. Carl F. Rehnborg, who was employed at different times by Carnation and Colgate in China, where he conducted studies on the impact of diets on the health of various Chinese populations. He found, for example, that rural Chinese, who ate more vegetables from their farms, were healthier than city dwellers, and that many Chinese suffered from osteoporosis because they drank little milk. He was impressed with the holistic wisdom of traditional Chinese culture and medicine. During an uprising in Shanghai in 1926, Carl was arrested for trying to help defend the city and was imprisoned. Confined to a fenced-in compound and a starvation diet, he looked for ways to maintain his health and prevent malnutrition. During his one-year imprisonment he made a soup of any green leafy vegetation he could find growing in the compound or that he could persuade guards to give him. He even added rusty nails to his stew, knowing the leached-out iron would add nutritional value. He remained healthier than most of the other prisoners.

After his release, he settled in San Pedro, California, where he held a variety of day jobs and worked on developing a plant-based nutritional supplement by night. In 1935, he quit his day job to work full-time making and distributing his new product. Realizing his product would require an explanation of its ingredients and benefits, he decided to sell his supplements himself rather than through stores. He started his own route of customers, and then recruited more salespeople, and within four years he named his company Nutrilite Products, Inc., and reported annual sales of $24,000. He was way ahead of his time.

I remember him being out in his organic farms with a big scythe harvesting the alfalfa that's a major ingredient in DOUBLE X supplements. Today, terms like *organic, antioxidants,* and *phytochemical* are familiar to people in the habit of taking daily vitamin supplements. Back then, such nutritional terms were familiar only to forward-thinking scientists like Carl.

But the nutritional benefit of the product was not enough of a selling point by itself to build a large business. The secret to Nutrilite's growing success was a new marketing plan that was the forerunner of what today is called multilevel marketing. The plan was the foundation for Amway and for the later success of many direct-selling companies that today have worldwide sales in the billions of dollars. Carl was more comfortable in his lab or on his farm, but he was called upon from time to time to speak at sales conventions, so he took a Dale Carnegie course to improve his speaking skills. It was in that class that he met a psychologist named William (Bill) Casselberry. Bill and his friend Lee Mytinger, a salesman, became NUTRILITE customers, but much more important, they developed a new multilevel marketing plan for selling the products. They formed Mytinger & Casselberry, Inc., which became the sales organization for Nutrilite Products, Inc.

When Jay and I started getting serious about our NUTRI-LITE supplements business, we actually fell back on some of our experience from our travelogue shows. We put ads in papers inviting people who might be interested in our products and our business opportunity and booked conference rooms in hotels or other public halls. Our presentations included a short film on nutrition. Jay typically welcomed our prospects, ran the projector, and answered questions. He mostly explained the benefits of the products while I encouraged people about the benefits of the business. We eventually drew larger and larger crowds.

Some of our early sales meetings, however, were disasters.

One time we ran ads on radio and in the newspapers and distributed brochures to build what we thought would be a large meeting in Lansing, Michigan. We rented a room with two hundred seats. Two people showed up. Little in my life would ever be as awkward as going through with a formal sales presentation to two people in a room that seated two hundred. On the drive back to Grand Rapids, Jay said, "If we can't do any better than that with all the publicity we did, maybe we should just drop the whole thing."

I was also feeling dejected, but because I didn't want Jay to be discouraged, I said, "We can't quit just because of one bad night. We know this can work." That was another lesson in persistence that I'd first learned selling vegetables with my grandfather.

We kept going, using both the sales meeting route and also a more personal approach of talking to everyone we knew about DOUBLE X supplements and the Nutrilite business. Our sales pitch was simple. "Just try it. People say it helps them feel better. Just try it for a year and see what happens." Out of twenty calls we might get four who were interested and maybe one who would buy. We always tried to convince each new customer to sign up for twelve months to give DOUBLE X a fair trial. Once a person was a customer, we explained to them the benefits of becoming a distributor. So not only were we approaching everyone we knew; our distributors were approaching everyone they knew and so on as they sponsored distributors.

The sting of those early meetings quickly evaporated as our business started to grow even beyond our expectations. We rented an office in the low-rent district of Grand Rapids for twenty-five dollars a month as our Ja-Ri Corporation headquarters. We put a sign in the window that said, YOU ARE WHAT YOU EAT. Some guy passing by asked, "So if I eat a banana, I'm a banana?" We laughed, but that reaction was typical for a time when most people were more interested in burgers, fries, and chocolate shakes at the drive-in than being concerned about nutrition and health.

Jay and I started to have fun and were very hands-on with our business. I remember borrowing chairs from funeral homes, which we loaded into a station wagon to take to one of the halls we rented, setting them up for a meeting, and taking them down the next morning to return to their owner.

A Nutrilite presentation took an hour to cover the nutritional benefits. We explained how farmers' soils had lost nutrients from years of growing crops, how products lost nutrition after being shipped and sitting on store shelves, how vegetables lost vitamins after being cooked in boiling water—all to convince customers of the value of supplementing their diets with additional vitamins and minerals. So we couldn't just walk up to people, show them the label on our box, and ask them to hand over a twenty-dollar bill. We had to be knowledgeable, convincing salesmen who knew the value of our products. Most people said no, but some bought, and one sales call even had a huge bonus for Jay. He called on a house in East Grand Rapids to try to make a sale, and the door was answered by a Mrs. Hoekstra. I remember Jay coming out of that house and saying, "Boy, they've got a nice-looking blond daughter in there." That blonde turned out to be his future wife, Betty.

———

WE EVENTUALLY STOPPED GOING door-to-door and making cold calls, because we had come to understand that ours was a person-to-person business. Instead we made lists of everyone we knew and asked them to refer people they knew, and started seeing customers by appointment. Once we made a sale, we returned to the customer every thirty days to sell them a new box of NU-TRILITE supplements after their thirty-day supply was gone. Instead of selling just one box, our goal was really to sell a lifetime supply, even though our customers were buying that supply one box at a time each month. Jay and I convinced our customers that taking NUTRILITE supplements month after month would help them realize the products' full benefits, and we impressed upon them that taking NUTRILITE supplements really should become a lifelong habit. (We were taking it ourselves, and I still am.)

We also would ask people to host meetings in their homes and invite as many people as they could think of—friends, relatives, neighbors, church members, coworkers, whomever. We suggested they announce they were going to have a meeting that could help everyone they knew start a new business—and to also let them know that they were in the business. Once we had an audience, the next key was to have someone they recognized who had an appealing personality, speaking skills, and was someone everyone trusted, to explain how the business works and its potential. Distributors we had sponsored in the business would bring their friends, and we would talk about the product.

It was not an easy sell. Twenty dollars was a huge amount of money in those days. So we had to sell not on price but on the high quality of the product—that it was natural and made from plants grown organically. We just had to overcome the price objection—like a salesman selling a new car to someone who thinks the price is too high, until he is sold on all the benefits and joys of driving a new car. Selling is never easy, but a good salesperson can find honest, convincing answers to most cost objections.

All sorts of people said it wouldn't work. It would never last. All the standard arguments against anything new. Doctors, especially, were opposed to us. Some told patients who were our customers, "You don't need any of that stuff; it's phony." Today, of course, daily vitamins and mineral supplements are accepted within the medical community. But in those days supplemental nutrition was frowned upon, not always because doctors doubted their value, but because we were intruding into their world. But if our customers saw the value of using NUTRILITE supplements, they really didn't care what their doctors said. So they kept on using them, and we kept on selling them. My parents became customers as soon as we did, as did Jay's parents. All four of them always were supportive.

We were making a living. We had a nice group started, and our business was strong enough that we could afford to buy another car. Sixty years ago, gas was about twenty cents a gallon and cars cost about a thousand dollars. It was a whole different world back then, and those kinds of numbers were considered big money.

In seeking new distributors, I'd diagram for potential distributors how many customers they would need, how big an organization they'd have to build for an income like ours. To motivate our distributors to succeed, we simply had to convince them that they *could* do it. And we found that the best way to convince them was to have other people talk about how they did it. We might have distributors who stuttered and stammered a bit—and were not the best speakers—but many times they were the best motivators, because people in the audience would think, "If he can do it, I can do it."

Within a few years our original group grew to a thousand, and it kept growing. We started holding conventions every spring at the Civic Auditorium in downtown Grand Rapids. Our program included both hired motivational speakers and our own distributors who had built successful businesses. For further motivation, we also brought onstage examples of the kind of lifestyles they could achieve by working hard and building their businesses. Beyond material incentives, we'd also talk about goals such as paying for a child's education at a private school, running their own businesses instead of just working jobs, or making additional income for a better life for themselves and their children. We eventually hosted five thousand members of our group at these conventions.

Sometimes when your dreams come true and success seems unstoppable, you hit a bump in the road. That's what happened to Nutrilite and our personal business. A key to our success had been the use of a brochure written by Casselberry titled *How to Get Well and Stay Well*, which described the importance of supplements in achieving optimal health. The Food and Drug Administration found many of the statements in the booklet to be "excessive claims" and brought a case against Nutrilite in 1948. The FDA had no understanding of the entrepreneurial side of the American people, or why they would sell these products. The FDA felt these products should be regulated like drugs.

The case eventually settled with a consent decree in 1951 listing several claims that were permissible to make about vitamins and minerals. Until then, there had been no official government position on what type of claims could be made about dictary supplements. With legislative changes in the 1990s, the dietary supplement industry obtained greater clarity in how to properly claim the benefits associated with vitamin and mineral supplements, and it is with this clarity and the lessons learned from the early days of the business that guide the claims we make about our products today. Nevertheless, the FDA case in 1948 had a significant impact and the Nutrilite business struggled as a result.

Because of the fallout from the FDA case, the Nutrilite company in California diversified to create a revenue source besides vitamins. They launched a line of cosmetics and started selling them directly to the distributors instead of going through Mytinger & Casselberry. That put into question the contract between Nutrilite Products, Inc., and Mytinger & Casselberry, Inc., as to which of the two actually owned the sales organization. So along with business slowing down because of the FDA controversy, we now were dealing with these internal squabbles. Mytinger and Casselberry were not getting along well with Carl Rehnborg or even with each other. They were against the idea of selling cosmetics and were losing the trust of distributors.

In 1958, Mytinger & Casselberry formed a study group of distributors to try to solve the problems and Jay was appointed chairman. Carl Rehnborg offered him the position of Nutrilite Products, Inc., president at a salary beyond his income at the time.

I called him and said, "Jay, if that's what you want to do, feel free. Don't let me get in your way on this thing."

Jay said, "What are you talking about?"

"Well, if that's something that's really important to you," I said, "I don't want to be an obstruction to you."

He said, "We're in business together! I'm your partner! I don't want to do anything apart from you!" That was a pretty powerful statement.

Jay turned down the position, telling me that being self-employed and in partnership with me was more important than a secure, steady income and the challenge of leading Nutrilite beyond its problems.

Jay and I now faced our own problems. What was our future with declining sales of our products and the internal squabbles threatening the existence of our product supplier? We had to consider the distributor organization under us, the thousands of people who relied on Nutrilite products for their livelihoods and future success. Regardless of the challenges, we were convinced we were in the right kind of business—that the foundation for our future lay in the people who had trusted us and the products and the business we presented. Besides, we knew that what we really were selling was an opportunity for people to succeed on their own and help others do the same through a unique marketing system.

All it took was the willingness to work hard to achieve a dream ranging from simply a better income to the freedom of owning a business. They didn't need to make a large investment or build a factory, or buy a warehouse of inventory or hire employees. All they needed was a commitment to succeed, hard work, and a desire to help other people succeed. I think this attitude may go back to my earliest days growing up in Grand Rapids. We shared a sense of community. People depended on each other. Neighbors wanted to be assured that their neighbors were providing for themselves and were happy and healthy. We lived close together, which encouraged us to get to know and appreciate one another. Neighbors conversed on front porches instead of retreating to decks in fenced backyards. I believe that's where my interest in people began and why I've been a people person all my life. I still love to meet new people, although I cherish old friends. What better foundation for a business than the talents and ambitions of people who also want what's best for others?

Whatever would happen to Nutrilite, Jay and I knew that the idea of people helping people to help themselves was a concept with great potential that we could build from. As long as the company and products had integrity, the real power lay in the sales plan and the ambition and dreams of people simply looking for an opportunity. We were convinced that we could make the opportunity even better by making people's rewards even greater. Our plans were about to unfold—on a long sheet of butcher paper rolled out on the floor of my kitchen.

PART TWO

SELLING AMERICA

CHAPTER FIVE

The American Way

THE AIR WAS FILLED with uncertainty and concern. Our livelihood—not to mention thousands of other independent Nutrilite distributors—depended on a large organization out in California that now was fractured and struggling. We faced a serious breakup between Mytinger & Casselberry, Inc.—which controlled the sales plan that compensated distributors—and Nutrilite Products, Inc.—the sole manufacturer of the products that distributors sold. Sales were falling after the new FDA restrictions, and both companies were trying to figure out what to do and how to lick it. They both concluded one answer might be to offer additional products, so Nutrilite introduced the EDITH REHNBORG line of cosmetics, named for the wife of Carl Rehnborg. But Mytinger & Casselberry decided they wanted to have just a face and skin care line instead of a full cosmetics line. They thought that would be simpler for distributors to manage, with fewer products and sizes. Mytinger & Casselberry were basically correct, if skin care products were all distributors had to offer, but they were not thinking beyond the moment. They didn't foresee how everything would change, that eventually distributors would be receiving their inventories from a manufacturer's central shipping points rather than picking up their own products as in the old days. Nutrilite decided to move forward selling their cosmetics line outside the Mytinger & Casselberry sales force. I think Carl Rehnborg was of the mind that we as independent distributors could simply sign up with his company and sell his new cosmetic line directly through Nutrilite.

With the insecurity of a manufacturer and distributor being at odds with each other, Jay and I decided the time had come for us to start a company that avoided these pitfalls and protected the distributor groups. We were confident we could at least get started by continuing to use the sales plan and marketing system that had helped us succeed as Nutrilite distributors. We would continue selling NUTRILITE products but also knew we would need to add a product or two of our own. We had long been touching on the subject of starting our own company of this type, and the time for that was now.

Jay and I at this point in our lives had personal reasons for needing to continue making a good living in a business of our own. We no longer were just two young buddies on an adventure together. By this time we both were married with children. You may recall from the last chapter that Jay had made a sales call at the house with the "nice-looking blond daughter"—he soon learned her name was Betty Jean Hoekstra, and I was the best man at their wedding in 1952. The following February, I married Helen Van Wesep, and by the time Jay and I began this new company, Helen and I were parents of two sons and Jay and Betty also had children to support. We had built houses next to each other near the rural village of Ada, Michigan, which one day would become Amway World Headquarters.

So we had more to consider than simply supporting ourselves, and we were far beyond the days when we could simply sell our business and go off on a sailing adventure. Looking back, we were taking an even greater risk in starting a new business than when we were young guys starting a flight school a dozen years earlier. Would people accept a new business based on the fledgling multilevel marketing system? Would independent distributors we sponsored into the Nutrilite business join us in our new venture? Could we find a new product line that customers would buy? I now can see how our early ventures were a solid foundation for facing these new uncertainties. Had we not started all those new businesses and set off on that sailing adventure, I'm not sure Jay and I would have even considered such a major new enterprise.

In the midst of all this uncertainty, we decided to make yet another leap of faith in our business lives. We had scheduled one of our regular retreats for our distributors and agreed this meeting would be our opportunity to announce our plans to start our own business. This would come as a great surprise to them, so by this being a regularly scheduled retreat we avoided the classic "I guess you're wondering why we called this meeting" situation.

We held the retreat in the summer of 1958 in Charlevoix, a small, picturesque resort town on Lake Michigan surrounded by other smaller lakes, woods, and dunes in the far north of Michigan's Lower Peninsula. We announced our plans and promised to anyone who wanted to join us that we would protect the business relationship between Nutrilite distributors in the line of sponsorship. We also formed a board of some of the top people in attendance who would join us in discussing this new venture and what it might look like.

As a name for our board, we settled on the American Way Association. We believed then—and still believe—that many people in this country would like a business of their own. We thought that was simply the American way. Surveys found that owning a business was a strong desire for most Americans, but few ever achieved that dream. So we wanted our new venture to be one that put people in businesses of their own but in which they would not be alone. They would have our support and the support of the Amway line of sponsorship. So that became our whole theme. What could be more American than to be free to own a business within the free enterprise system that had powered America's economic system from its beginnings? The name American Way Association eventually became a little too long to handle, so we kept that name for the board and operated as a company under the shortened name Amway.

It all really began at that meeting in Charlevoix with some of the distributors we directly sponsored. We worked with them and charted out the idea, and threw it out on the floor to see what they thought about it. These people were independent distributors, not our employees, so they were free to join us or walk away. They all said they would support our new venture and join us in this new effort, although it was anything but a sure thing. Jay and I had become used to rejection from our early days trying to build our business, but in this case, not a single person walked out of the meeting and we were gratified by their response. Many in that core group went on to become some of the most successful Amway distributors for decades, and today, many of their children are leaders in the business.

I think this was a key lesson for us about the true meaning of leadership. For one thing, Jay and I decided that it was essential for us to lead, and we must have the courage to lead. The fact that everyone followed also was meaningful. I believe they followed not only because they respected Jay and me, but because our asking them to join us showed that we respected them. To this day, I firmly believe that effective leaders only truly gain respect by showing respect.

Of course, if we planned to expand our product line, the big question at our retreat was "What products are we going to sell?" Our retreat in Charlevoix was also where we came up with the answer. We mentioned to the group that we were looking for products and invited their suggestions. One of our distributors spoke up and said he knew of an all-purpose cleaner called FRISK, which was made by a small manufacturer in Detroit. Because he knew one of the guys who made the product, he made a visit to their manufacturing plant, talked to him, and brought back some samples. Some of our distributors started using FRISK all-purpose cleaner and sharing it with some of their customers. They all liked it, so we started ordering the product and having it shipped from Detroit to Ada.

The basements of our homes in Ada became the first office and warehouse of Amway. Most people today who drive over a crest of a hill and see the mile-long Amway World Headquarters, with its offices and manufacturing plants, likely don't realize that Amway was started in this rural area simply by accident. When Jay and I were still single, we decided to look for property where we might build our houses next to each other, thinking we'd get married sometime and raise families. We found this very pleasant spot on a hill overlooking a river and decided to buy a couple of lots. It was a while after buying the land that we were married, but our wives, Helen and Betty, generously accepted the fact that they never really had a choice about where they would live. And because that was where we lived, it was in that community where Amway began.

Ada is about five miles east of Grand Rapids and even today is a small village in a rural community. It is still a typical small town, with a covered bridge, treelined residential streets, and shops along a couple of streets that intersect. When we started Amway, the area must have seemed to many to be in the middle of nowhere. This may have appealed to a desire for rural living that I had expressed as early as the eighth grade. Interestingly, I was in a debate class then and once was assigned the topic of the merits of country versus city living. I took the side of living in the country. I used Ada as my example: where the river ran through, an ideal place to live and raise children, in the country but not too far away from the city of Grand Rapids. Of course, as a schoolkid, I never could have known that one day I'd actually build both a home and a business in Ada.

When we started Amway, my basement was the warehouse and Jay's was the office. We shared one business phone line and used a buzzer to alert each other when to pick up. Helen knew how to type and helped with secretarial duties until we hired a part-time secretary as our first employee. Jay wrote sales literature and a monthly newsletter on a Smith Corona manual typewriter, printed copies on a mimeograph machine, and collated the literature on his Ping-Pong table. Once our sales manual grew, Jay hired the young man who mowed his lawn to do the collating—and eventually he was the one who ran Amway's first print shop. We also hired two more employees to help me process orders, keep sales records, and pay the bonuses.

Helen thumbtacked yards of muslin, which her Brownie Girl

Scout troop had tie-dyed in pink, over the bare stud walls in an unfinished room downstairs that had become my office. But even this "fancying-up" couldn't hide the fact that our corporate headquarters was still just a basement room with my used metal desk and office chair next to cartons of FRISK stacked on the floor. I recall this as a very happy time, because we were at the start of building something. I don't think I looked much beyond the possibility of Amway outgrowing our basements—I just felt grateful to be growing our own business in our homes and hopeful of a possible bright future for Amway. I also appreciate, now more than ever, Helen and her role in the early days. She probably was wondering what she had gotten herself into with a business being run out of her basement, but she gamely joined in the adventure.

Distributors were picking up FRISK from my basement; I had a porch glider in the basement that could double as a bed, and distributors coming from Ohio to pick up products or show the Sales Plan to prospects in Michigan would occasionally sleep there overnight. We would ship a few orders principally within Michigan and Ohio, and our washer and dryer tops would double as a table to package orders for shipping. With increasing sales volume, Jay and I realized that we needed to move from simply filling orders for product—we really had to control the source and quality of the products we sold, which meant we would need to become manufacturers as well as distributors.

On Fulton Street, the highway that runs past Ada less than a mile from our homes, was a white brick service station with two gas pumps on a dirt parking lot. The station sold gasoline to farmers and serviced farm equipment. We bought the sixty-by-forty-foot building and its two acres and moved our manufacturing operation in. We also decided to buy two additional acres adjoining the property because I told Jay at the time, "We might someday have the need for additional parking." The building also had room for warehousing and an office for me. In back was a bathroom, which, when combined with a bed, became the home of a young man who was one of our first employees and who managed our first warehouse. We also hired a young man from the neighborhood as our sign painter. He painted our AMWAY name on the building with the words PRODUCTS FOR HOME AND INDUSTRY and even added the American Way Association logo. This was our first visible company, where our first product was manufactured, distributors picked up product, and the public passing by noticed the start of a new business in the neighborhood.

FRISK, which we soon thereafter renamed L.O.C., Liquid Organic Cleaner, turned out to be a winner as our first product and helped set the stage for more products to come. For one thing, it was made from natural coconut oil derivatives instead of from a petroleum-based product such as kerosene. An early promotional brochure showed L.O.C. being used to clean vegetables. L.O.C. also had unique cleaning ability—removing dirt and stains that other products would not. It was a great cleaning product, and we sold a lot of it. We also were at the beginning of an era of growing interest in natural and organic ingredients. Petroleum-based products were gaining a bad reputation and phosphates were harming waterways. Wastewater from detergents in sinks and washing machines were foaming in rivers and streams and being blamed for harm to wildlife and the environment. Our product was biodegradable, and because we used a concentrated formula to reduce both shipping and storage volume, our product used less packaging—an environmental benefit not truly appreciated until decades later. Our next product, a laundry detergent called SA8, also used biodegradable surfactants and was concentrated. Just as we were far ahead of nutritional trends with NUTRILITE products, we now were ahead of environmental trends with AMWAY products.

In keeping with our American Way theme, we also had our packaging designed with red, white, and blue colors. We were accused by critics of wrapping our products in the American flag. Our logo was simple: the word AMWAY in a font that appeared as if it had just been pulled from a typewriter. Our packaging also included our original slogan—"Home Care Know How *at your doorstep!*"

After adding a few more home care products, we quickly became known—perhaps critically by some—as a "soap" company. I was asked to defend our strategy, and as I told distributors: "Soap. Why does Amway sell it? Simple. Everybody uses soap. They use it up. And then they buy more. They don't need to get samples to understand soap, and they buy it without risk because it carries a satisfaction guarantee." But even with a product as simple as L.O.C., we still encouraged distributors to use the products themselves and then demonstrate to their prospective customers how well the products worked for them. Jay even wrote a piece of sales literature called "The Amazing FRISK Story."

We urged distributors not to just *tell* prospects how good AMWAY products are, but also to *show* them. The ability to buy products from friends, and have them demonstrated and delivered to your door, added value for customers and we considered them unique features of our style of business.

Even as our manufacturing operation grew with the rising popularity of L.O.C. all-purpose cleaners and SA8 detergents and the introduction of new products—including a shoe spray, concrete floor cleaner, furniture polish, and car wax—Jay and I still had to hit the road to recruit new distributors. In the early 1960s, I was traveling to distributor meetings from New York to Washington and Texas to Manitoba and all states in between. We kept our eye primarily on getting customers who potentially would quickly become distributors. There was rejoicing when we signed up somebody new, rejoicing when we got a customer, and rejoicing when a distributor got his customer.

From our experience as distributors, Jay and I knew that the sales plan developed by Mytinger & Casselberry could be improved to better reward distributors based on their level of achievement. After many discussions and getting input from our distributors, in 1959, on my kitchen floor, Jay and I rolled out a large piece of butcher paper and started to diagram a unique plan that rewarded those who produced the volume. Our plan fairly rewarded distributors for not only their individual sales volume and the volume for each distributor they personally sponsored, but also further down for the sales volume of the people they sponsored and in turn sponsored.

When you imagine the number of people who could eventually become a part of the Amway line of sponsorship, you can appreciate why we needed the roll of butcher paper, which was running out of the kitchen and down the hall as we kept writing; and perhaps can even picture Jay and me on the floor, diagramming this complicated plan. Of course, back in 1959, we could never have imagined the day when compensating millions of distributors would require sophisticated computers that had not yet been invented. Still, we were dreaming big.

Our plan was designed to move commissions downward from one level to the next and keep the money moving to the two-hundredth level or to as many levels to which a business might grow. We dreamed that someday there could be a thousand people in one leg of the Amway line of sponsorship. Where does that money end up? That's why we needed a roll of paper to write it all down.

We called the plan we designed the "pass-through" system. The "pass-through" plan was one of the keystones of our business that ensured distributor compensation would be equitable and proportionate to their sales volume and the volume of downline distributor groups. Along with the plan we also worked with the board to develop bonus amounts for levels of achievement in sponsoring and sales volume. We established the pin levels that still are used today—Pearl, Emerald, Diamond, etc. We needed to have a track of upward success that was meaningful, yet short and simple. We planned to present pins to distributors when they achieved each new level of achievement, so jewel names just made sense and added a little pizzazz to the recognition.

The appeal of Amway in the early days was the same as today. People are attracted by the possibility of owning a business and gravitate to an actual opportunity with large potential but one that requires only a few dollars of start-up capital. They wouldn't need to invest in manufacturing or warehousing inventory, yet would have easy access to hundreds of products to sell. They also would have earning rights to the people they bring into the business. So they have a multiplication factor of income from not only what they sell but also the sales of those they sponsor and everyone else then sponsored by others into their sales organization.

Finally, they own their business, which they one day can sell or pass on to their children. So, if there is any secret to the success of Amway, I believe it was our confidence in people and their abilities to use their efforts and talents to achieve their dreams. I'm not certain how grateful I was at the time to all these early distributors. But looking back, I marvel at them—their dedication to a new, untested venture, their faith in Jay and me, their perseverance in the face of some rejection at times. I'm so grateful for each one of them and feel blessed that they came along and joined us.

We never separated doing business within the free enterprise system from the blessings of freedom we enjoyed in America. We proudly called our business the American Way and never apologized for our belief in free enterprise or our patriotism as free Americans. We started Amway the same year that Fidel Castro took over Cuba. Two years earlier, the Soviet Union had launched its Sputnik satellite into orbit, and early in 1961 they had orbited a man in space. It's hard to imagine now, but citizens of the United States—who won World War II to preserve their American freedoms and way of life—were seriously wondering if they were taking second place to communism. People thought communism could be the wave of the future and might even overtake America. When we started Amway, we thought, "It's okay to start a business to make money, but what's the ultimate purpose of our business? What does it stand for? What's driving it emotionally beyond just trying to make money?" So "Standing Up for Free Enterprise" was our battle cry.

When we thought about owning our own business, we thought the opportunity to do so was fundamental to America. We thought *everyone* who wanted to should be able to own their own business! I would go on to espouse free enterprise in my first book, *Believe!*, and tout our American economic system to millions in my speech "Selling America."

I was not espousing a theory. My belief in free enterprise, and my defense of free enterprise as the greatest economic engine the world has ever known, was borne out daily as we watched our little business grow. A vacant floodplain in a tiny rural village began to rapidly sprout manufacturing plants, warehouses, and offices. Here was the overwhelming evidence of the power of free enterprise, something that even all my speeches and writings could not measure up to—what is today the Amway World Headquarters.

CHAPTER SIX

Powered by People

THE COMMON BUYER-BEWARE JOKE is the one about never falling for the sales pitch about great real estate in Florida (which could turn out to be swampland). By this time in our careers, Jay and I were too smart to mistakenly buy property sight unseen, but we did decide to buy, if not swampland, at least lowland in a floodplain! The property, bought in parcels over time, eventually became the site of Amway.

Not far from our homes in Ada, fronting Fulton Street, the main highway through the village, were hundreds of acres of pristine vacant land. We originally bought on this site the small parcel with the old service station that now was the home of Amway Manufacturing Corporation. We could not have known at the time that we one day would need to buy all three hundred acres as Amway expanded. Fortunately for us, the land was not highly desirable for development and had remained vacant for many years until we needed the acreage. The property ran along the Grand River, and much of the land was in a floodplain, making it unsuitable for building. So as we expanded, we needed to first excavate some of the dirt to use as fill for each construction site. The giant hole left from all that digging filled with water and ever since has been known as "Lake Amway" to all Amway employees.

Within a year of our locating in the former service station in 1960, we started a construction project on the two acres that we thought we might one day need for parking. On that property we built our first office building, a showplace at the time, of flagstone and plate-glass windows. The headline in our distributor newsletter, the *Amagram,* blared: "Staff Moves into Stunning Setting of Glass & Stone."

We erected a huge sign out front in red, white, and blue with our new logo and slogan. This also was the occasion for me to visit the Steelcase office furniture dealer in Grand Rapids to buy my first brand-new desk and chair. Our first office building is still among the structures that comprise Amway's operations in Ada—which today stretch a mile along Fulton Street. Hidden somewhere in the interior of that giant complex is a wall from the old service station.

Construction of our first office building was a key decision. At the time, we thought we had built our last executive office building, a quality project that would meet our needs forever—the office building to end all office buildings. Jay and I were still in our mid-thirties, and we'd just built an impressive project for those days. We were proud of it; this was a milestone in our careers. The building was also the physical representation of Amway and symbol of our growing success. Jay and I had offices next to each other and an adjoining conference room. Our business kept growing, which meant we had to keep building—so we stayed with our plan of keeping administration buildings fronting Fulton Street, and warehouses and manufacturing plants behind them. (Eventually, with manufacturing plants for aerosols, powders, liquids, cosmetics, and plastic bottles; research and development buildings; distribution and transportation centers; and administrative buildings for thousands of employees, we had 4.2 million square feet under our roof.) After our first full year of Amway, we reported sales of $500,000. Just three years later, 1963 sales were $21 million.

Once I discovered we had a tour guide who was telling visitors, "We're going to do one hundred million dollars just like nothing." I took him aside and said, "Wait a minute. Nobody in this industry has ever reached one hundred million. So let's just be a little careful about what we say around here." I couldn't shake his confidence, but I told him, "Let's just not over brag about ourselves at the moment. Let's just talk about what we really have, not what you think it's going to be. I'm just asking you not to use that number anymore." It was when we *did* reach that $100 million mark in 1970 that Jay and I could finally admit to ourselves that this thing could be really big and that we needed to expand our thinking and planning to accommodate the growth. Things were moving so fast, I don't recall spending a lot of time dwelling on our sales numbers. What we did spend time on was hiring people who could help us in this expansion, from book-keepers to researchers, people who would provide the expertise we needed right then.

All our revenues in those days were reinvested into growing the business. I don't recall spending a lot on ourselves or trying to impress people or acting like big shots. I think we still just con-sidered ourselves hardworking business guys trying to make a living.

My dad, who had retired, was our first tour guide. At the time we only had forty square feet of office space, and maybe sixty feet behind that was just an open concrete pad where we kept raw materials outside. We didn't have an enclosed warehouse, because all we could afford were the walls without a roof. We just threw tarps over the barrels of materials. We would wheel that stuff into the factory, measure it out, and pour it in to make our L.O.C. or whatever else we were producing at that time. There wasn't much to see in those early days, but my dad became the tour guide be-cause there were always distributors and other people coming around who wanted to see the operation. So my dad would visit with them and show them what was going on. But the best part for me was that he lived long enough, before his fatal heart attack at age fifty-nine, to see the beginning of this company. And he never stopped encouraging me along the way. I'll never forget what he said to me once during those early days. He had given careful thought about what he wanted to express to me and spent several minutes with me to ensure that I understood and appreciated his point of view.

"This thing is really becoming something," he told me. "It's going to be big. You're making a lot of promises to these people about how things are going to go and what you're going to do. Don't forget you need to be living up to these promises. You must honor them! So I'm charging you to remember what you have promised people you will do and make sure you keep on doing it. This thing is rolling so fast and is going to be so big that the things you do today and the things you set in place today are going to be very important. God has blessed you and you're going to be held accountable for your promises."

That was a precious time for me—hearing my dad's wise and caring words. He had given it careful thought and just wanted us to sit down for a few minutes so he could tell me how he felt about the future of this business and the importance of keeping our promises. He did not live to see Amway grow to substantial success, unfortunately. But I always knew how proud of me he was, because he told me so. I think he was proud of me simply for having the confidence and skills to fulfill his dream of my owning a business.

As a father, I now know how important it is to tell our children that we are proud of them. Our pride gives them the confidence to face challenges and succeed on their own. I would never have been able to repay the debt I owed my father for the simple yet remarkable role he played in my life by encouraging me and showing that he was proud of me. I continue to try to do the same with my children.

Even as our rapid growth was getting under way, we were beginning to sense that people were starting to pay attention to our success and that Amway was becoming a household name nationwide. I think the first time that struck me was when Paul Harvey asked to visit Amway. In the early 1960s, Paul Harvey was famous and had a huge following for his *Paul Harvey News and Commentary* program, which was broadcast daily on radio stations nationwide. He also was famous for his on-air readings of the advertisements of his program's sponsors.

Amway had no advertising agency in those early days, but we liked Paul Harvey and were considering sponsoring his radio program. Paul Harvey came to visit, and he said to Jay and me, "You guys said Amway started in a basement. Where's that basement?" I called Helen to let her know so she would be prepared for his arrival. We drove Paul Harvey to my house and took him downstairs to the corner room that had been my original office and Amway warehouse. He liked this idea of a couple of guys starting a new business. That intrigued him. We began advertising on his show, with Paul writing the scripts for our ads and reading them on the air. It was kind of a grassroots advertising that was really very simple. He would ad-lib a little, tell stories about the company, and include flattering references.

In fact, he came up with our second slogan. During one of his sales pitches on the air he ad-libbed the comment, "Shop Without Going Shopping." That became the slogan printed with our logo beginning in 1964 and used for almost two decades. He helped establish our business. He also spoke at many Amway conventions. Whenever he appeared onstage, his clothing was impeccable. Knowing he flew privately on a Learjet for hours at a time, we once asked him how he managed to look so good. The answer? He told us that when traveling between meetings he would take off his trousers and hang them up so they wouldn't get wrinkled and then put them back on just before he landed. Jay and I always had a lot of fun teasing him about flying in his boxer shorts.

Another promotion that helped build awareness for Amway was our advertisements in the *Saturday Evening Post,* which included portraits of Jay and me drawn by Norman Rockwell. We advertised in the *Post* principally because we were friends with the owners of the magazine at the time, and they encouraged us to advertise and have Rockwell do our portraits from photographs that we provided.

Just as having Paul Harvey say nice things about Amway in the early 1960s was a big deal, I think our Rockwell portraits in the *Saturday Evening Post* also added value to the Amway story. We did sponsor some radio and TV shows in the early 1980s voiced by Bob "Speaking for Amway" Hope, yet I think we learned in the end that our best promoters were Amway distributors.

Amway kept growing with the number of new distributors who in turn sponsored more new distributors into the business. But Jay and I also knew that our business could not truly grow unless this growing army of distributors had more and more products to sell. So product development was the focus for our fledgling business. We started with household cleaning products, because they were used by everyone and were used rather quickly, which led to repeat sales. Every product we introduced increased our sales volume. Once an available number of distributors sell their customers their available product line, what can they do next to increase their volume? So we worked hard at introducing new products all the time. We started a department to focus solely on research and development of new products.

Within the first eight years of Amway, we were selling one hundred different products nationwide.

A line of quality products with some unique qualities and a satisfaction guarantee also provided something tangible for distributors who had no storefronts or corporate buildings to promote themselves through as business owners. Products also were a means of promoting Amway at a time when the company had only a small manufacturing plant and office building in a village that no one beyond West Michigan had ever heard of.

At a time when the common responses were "Who ever heard of Ada? Who ever heard of Amway?" we had what we thought was an intriguing solution. We bought a bus from a guy we knew in Grand Rapids and had it painted red, white, and blue. We added the name AMWAY SHOWCASE and the message UNUSUAL IDEAS ON THE CARE OF YOUR HOME. The bus greeted the curious with the message EVERYONE WELCOME. FREE EXHIBIT.

We hired a driver to take that bus around the country and park it at downtown street corners or other high-traffic areas. Distributors took their customers through for tours to see our products, the exhibits that showed how the products were made, and product demonstrations. Looking back, I don't know how much overall impact the showcase bus had on our business. But that unique-looking vehicle gave distributors, who were lone souls out there representing a little-known company, a means to show there was something substantial behind them.

For distributors to do well, we knew they had to have a good product line they could sell. The bus was part of doing whatever we could to help support them in their businesses. The theory always was that if we help them do better, we'll do better. Distributors would say, "Nobody knows me, nobody's ever heard of the company, they question if we really exist," and so forth. The bus was a way to give them proof that we did exist. It was an important sales and marketing tool. Looking back, I think Jay and I were always seeking ways to support distributors in gratitude for their dedication to us and our business. After all, they were taking a chance on us. Their livelihoods depended on Amway succeeding and growing. And we depended on them succeeding to help us grow. We couldn't let them down.

We also toyed with the idea of distributors having regular product-delivery routes. I think we were still of the mind that to have a good Amway business, we needed to be like the neighborhood milkman who called on the same customers regularly. That brought up an interesting point of discussion: "Is Amway a product business or a distributor business?" As we grew, we realized products were important, but just as important, if not more so, was the appeal of the distributor business. The unique focus of Amway was distributors building their own businesses by selling products and sponsoring others to do the same. We put in place rules to teach distributors the importance of a balanced business with both selling and sponsoring. Product sales are essential for making money in Amway, but a focus on products wasn't where the business was going at that time. So we realized that success required both product sales and the opportunity for distributors to give new people the opportunity to build their own business through sponsoring others and then helping them succeed at selling and sponsoring.

To help distributors succeed, the bulk of what I was doing was holding meetings around the country. A distributor in Phoenix, for example, might be meeting with a few prospects in his home, so I would go to Phoenix and run a recruiting meeting for their invited guests. I'd tell the story of Amway, and hopefully they'd sign up some of the people who came. Attendance at the meeting ranged from a few to a few dozen, and even into the hundreds, depending on how well Amway was established in a community. We also relied for our early success on Nutrilite distributors who were interested in starting Amway businesses and who already had large groups of distributors in their Nutrilite business. This was especially helpful in reaching far beyond Ada to build a national business.

We were building Amway in the same way we had built our Nutrilite business—a network of relationships that begins with one person and keeps expanding. Some of the most successful Amway distributors in history began as Nutrilite distributors whom Jay and I sponsored, and they in turn built their businesses in the Amway line of sponsorship numbering into the tens of thousands.

In the early days, we sponsored Walter Bass, whom we met when he was sales manager for WOOD Radio, one of the largest stations in Grand Rapids. Walter got his hair cut in the basement of a Grand Rapids hotel by his barber, named Fred Hansen. Walter sponsored Fred and his wife, Bernice, into the Amway business. Later the Hansens moved to Cuyahoga Falls, Ohio, to sell house trailers. Walter and I drove there and held a recruiting meeting in their living room with about a half dozen people. The Hansens then sponsored their milkman, Jere Dutt, who then sponsored a fellow milkman, Joe Victor. Jere also knew a guy who worked in a prison in Rome, New York, by the name of Charlie Marsh, and sponsored him. So not only did these early activities and relationships lead to some of the most successful people ever in the Amway business, they also led to Amway's reach extending from Michigan into Ohio and then into New York State.

An aside to this story is the origin of circle drawing. Everyone in Amway is familiar with how distributors present the Sales

Plan by drawing circles. The presenter at a meeting first draws a circle representing a person who might be interested in becoming an Amway distributor. Lines are drawn from that primary circle to other circles representing people the prospective distributor might sponsor. Then lines are drawn extending from those secondary circles to others representing people they might sponsor. So the drawing represents an expanding web of people joining in a growing business. (Charlie Marsh may not have been the first to use the circle approach, but apparently he had done so with such flair that he had gained a reputation as the first distributor to draw the circles.)

It's amazing how much power in the Amway business came out of Cuyahoga Falls, Ohio, and Rome, New York. In fact, meetings in Cuyahoga were growing into the thousands, and were too big for me to pass up. Helen still needles me because on the way home from our honeymoon I insisted that we stop to attend a meeting in Cuyahoga.

At another Ohio meeting, another important Amway tradition began. I was asked to introduce Jere Dutt at a meeting in Canton that was attended by about three to four thousand people. I introduced him first and, separately, I introduced his wife. Jere later pulled me aside and said, "You're doing the introduction wrong. It's Jere *and* Eileen Dutt. We need to recognize Eileen as an equal partner in this business." That was a sound piece of advice. And that's how we refer in spoken introductions and print to all married couples in the business to this day. Jere and Eileen, by the way, became Amway's first Diamond Direct Distributors in 1964, which at that time was the highest level of achievement in the Amway business.

Sometimes you just don't know how or where seeds planted at even a small meeting might one day bear fruit. That little meeting in Phoenix I mentioned earlier is a great example. A while later I was at a meeting near the Nutrilite headquarters in Buena Park, California. A guy who had been at the Phoenix meeting rode down on a bus from San Francisco to attend. He was hanging around outside the room and said, "I don't know if I'm allowed in the meeting."

I said, "Are you going to get in the business?"

"Oh yeah," he said.

"Well, then come on in!" I said.

After the meeting he signed up and wrote a check to buy the sales kit. As he left he told me, "Don't cash that check until at least Monday, because I won't be able to get back home till then to deposit my paycheck."

The next time I came through his area I held a meeting in his garage. They had some planks set up on boxes of SA8 detergent as seating for about a dozen people. That was our first meeting in Northern California and the beginning of the business of Frank and Rita Delisle, who went from not having enough in the bank to cover a check for a sales kit to building a huge distributor organization.

I was on the road and away from my family a lot in these days. But I don't recall my travels and meeting with distributors as work. This, again, was where my natural love of being with people came into play. I was simply fascinated by meeting with all these enthusiastic, positive people and marveled at how their ambition was growing a huge business across the country. I never lost sight of the fact that they were the heart of the business.

By 1972, our business was booming, with $180 million in annual sales. But one thing was missing. As former Nutrilite distributors, we knew we needed to own a line of nutritional products if we wanted to keep growing at this pace. We knew Nutrilite made the best nutritional supplements, so we called them to see if they were interested in selling the business. When Jay and I were selling their products in the 1950s we thought Nutrilite was a huge company. But even by 1972, their annual sales were still only about $25 million, so in comparison with what we were doing, Nutrilite no longer looked as impressive.

We spoke with Carl Rehnborg and told him, "We'd like to add your whole line to ours. What do you think?" Surprisingly, he said, "Let's talk." Carl had hired a team to help him run his company, but Nutrilite was not the robust business it had been. The guys he hired to run the company couldn't figure out how to get it to go, so they thought selling was worth discussing. We arrived at what we thought was a fair number, offered a deal, and went to California to sign it. Carl, along with his family and some of his staff, took us to his club to celebrate that the Nutrilite company now was owned by Amway.

But the reality hit when we had to go and meet with the top distributors of NUTRILITE products.

During the thirteen years since the founding of Amway,

there'd been some competition, and some of the Nutrilite distributors had become Amway distributors. Some in Nutrilite saw us as cutting into their business and stealing their distributors. So to this group of top Nutrilite distributors at the meeting, we were not Amway. Many referred to us as "Damnway." We arrived in this meeting room of about two hundred Nutrilite distributors who had been called by the company to attend this special gathering. Carl's son, Sam, who worked closely with his father in the business, announced that they had sold to somebody who promised to keep the marketing plan going and maybe improve it.

Then he introduced the new owners—Jay and me.

While I don't remember hearing any boos, I know we didn't hear any applause. They were stunned. I can still picture that meeting: Jay and I standing in front of this crowd all alone and feeling a bit exposed to their stares and looks of resentment. We didn't have many friends there that day. But we started telling them how we planned to combine the two companies and how we were going to bring the whole group back together. Where there were conflicts, we promised we would sit down and resolve them. We said we would make a better business for them. But that was a tough meeting. Afterward some of them came up to us to talk, and we told them about our Amway business and how well it was doing. They couldn't believe our size or how far we'd come.

———

MY JOB WAS TO be on the road—making presentations, attending or staging conventions, honoring requests to speak at distributor meetings. I would usually schedule a trip across the country and just hit towns where we had reasonable numbers of distributors. Distributors were holding meetings regularly anyway, and I was invited to be the guest speaker. In other cities, Amway staff would set up meetings where I would speak. That reminds me of something else Jere Dutt told me when he invited me to speak at one of his large meetings in Cuyahoga.

I said, "What do you want me to talk about? You want me to talk about Amway?"

Jere answered, "No. Talk about freedom and free enterprise! That's what we want to hear about. We know all about Amway. We can tell that story. But you teach us *why* we do this. Why we are working so hard to build these businesses of our own, why it's important to us and to our country. We want to feel that we're making the world a better place by helping others."

So that's what I talked about, and that essentially became a strong message for all my talks to distributors. The opportunity in Free America. How, with a little money but a big vision of what you can achieve by working hard, working on your own, and getting it done, you can succeed. Sounds like an Amway distributor, doesn't it? These talks became the framework of my most memorable speeches, such as "The Four Stages," "Try or Cry," and "The Four Winds."

And then out of the blue came another setback. The family was on our boat in Northern Michigan in the summer of 1969 when I received a call late in the evening that our aerosol plant had burst into flames. Jay was at home and heard what he later said he thought was a sonic boom. The explosion turned the sky red over Ada that July evening. We flew home early the next morning to see that the aerosol plant had turned to ashes. Thankfully, there were no deaths, and the seventeen employees who had been burned were treated and all eventually released from the hospital. Firefighters kept the blaze from destroying the rest of our complex.

Just as we had moved on after our sailboat sank, or when our early Nutrilite efforts produced more rejections than sales, we decided to pick ourselves up, dust ourselves off, and start again. The decision was obvious. It was time to move on. That was the lesson we had been presenting to distributors for years. We could hardly do otherwise. We had promises to keep. My father had told me to keep my promises to people who would come to depend on Amway, and that advice has stayed with me to this day.

Beyond the millions of square feet of buildings constructed and the hundreds of products developed, the success and essence of Amway remains the talents and achievements of people working together. We thought for a short while that our new Amway business was all about developing and selling products. Quality products are essential, but we learned that our distributors were energized by something more—the opportunity to succeed in a business of their own through their own efforts, perseverance, and belief in themselves. That's why in those early meetings I was asked by distributors not to talk only about the Amway business, but about principles of optimism and perseverance. I told them, "You can do it! I believe in you!" Amway has always been powered by people who believe they can do it and believe others can do it, too. That's why the number of Amway distributors grew so quickly from Ada, Michigan, to Cuyahoga Falls, Ohio, to Rome, to New York, to California, and eventually around the world.

In light of their overwhelming belief and effort, a plant destroyed by fire could hardly have stopped us. By this time, overcoming challenges had become a way of life and business. But little did we suspect at the time that we would face and overcome much larger challenges.

CHAPTER SEVEN

The Critics Weigh In

A s THE OLD DUTCH saying goes, "The tallest tulip is the one that's cut." With Amway's phenomenal growth, we had grown very tall and no longer could escape the notice of those who might be wondering just what this unusual and surprisingly successful enterprise was up to—or maybe even wanting to cut us down. By 1975, Amway was reporting annual sales of $250 million; had opened overseas markets in Australia, the United Kingdom, Hong Kong, and Germany; had a corporate yacht and a fleet of jets; and added ARTISTRY cosmetics, AMWAY Queen cookware, and SATINIQUE personal care products to its home care and NUTRILITE product lines. Even as Jay and I were kneeling over that length of butcher paper in my kitchen back in 1959, coming up with a novel Sales Plan for our fledgling venture called Amway, we might have imagined that one day our plan would come under scrutiny by those who found us suspect. After all, we already had been through ten years of a novel Nutrilite business and had even been challenged by the Food and Drug Administration.

Amway had started to grow very quickly and was beginning to be noticed. People were confused about how this business of "you sponsor someone and that someone sponsors others" worked and they may also have been skeptical of our legitimacy. At the time, direct selling and multilevel marketing were suspect. In the public's eyes, Amway was typically not the company but instead the person next door who was selling Amway products as an independent distributor. Because of our multilevel marketing approach, some people mistakenly thought this type of business had the makings of a pyramid.

This sentiment became reality in 1975 when the Federal Trade Commission filed an official complaint against Amway. The FTC charged that the Amway Sales Plan was a "scheme to pyramid distributors upon ever-increasing numbers of other distributors," that it was "doomed to failure," and that it contained an "intolerable potential to deceive." They claimed we were price fixing by telling distributors at what prices they could sell their products, that we were restricting the activities of distributors by preventing them from selling AMWAY products through retail stores, and charged us with misrepresenting the potential opportunities for success.

These charges threatened the very future of Amway. But we knew we were in the right. So our first reaction was, "We're going to fight it." And we did, for the next two and a half years, including six months of hearings before an administrative law judge. It's hard to win a war with the government, because they've got unlimited time and money, so their attorneys can keep fighting. When they had me on the stand, they questioned me about testimony they had from ex-distributors who claimed they had been promised that they could make a thousand dollars a month but hadn't made anything.

The FTC started building its case by asking for the names of all Amway distributors. Letters were sent to distributors to solicit testimony from any who hadn't achieved their dreams. A number of people were happy to do that. So the FTC had a lineup of ex-distributors who were disgruntled for one reason or another. They dredged up anybody who was unhappy with Amway and screened them to come up with who they thought might make the best witnesses on the stand and have the strongest case against us.

When an ex-distributor took the stand, I'd say to my attorney, "Ask him what he did before he got in and what he's doing now." In most cases, they had improved their lives. They might not have stayed in Amway, but they ended up benefiting from trying to have a business of their own and were doing significantly better than before. In fact, when asked, they admitted they were doing a lot better. When our attorney asked them why, they admitted it was because of what Amway had taught them about running a business, selling products, setting goals, motivating themselves, and working with people. To which our attorney could then say, "Thank you. No further questions." So we showed that we promoted success in Amway coming only with effort and that even the people who had not done well in Amway or had not stuck with Amway had a great improvement in their lives.

The FTC ruled that our plan was *not* a pyramid scheme, because compensation is based entirely on the sale of products to end-user consumers, rather than for recruiting new participants. As a result of the FTC's decision, the AMWAY Sales Plan became the model for a legitimate direct-selling business. Other direct-selling companies have been trying to copy us ever since. The commission even pointed out that our products enjoyed great consumer acceptance and even were third in brand loyalty despite our small market share and no national advertising. The FTC recognized that we had developed something new and exciting. Faced with industry giants like Procter & Gamble, which spent more than twice as much on advertising as Amway's total sales, our distributors introduced a "vigorous new competitive presence," winning business from the huge companies that dominated the market. The commission found that the AMWAY Sales Plan makes clear the idea that work will be involved and that material rewards depend on the amount and quality of work. One judge even shared with me after the suit was settled that he thought the AMWAY Sales Plan was a truly new and unique business model.

Our case with the FTC set the standard for what was a legitimate multilevel marketing business. That suit was the test case that set the standards and guidelines by which all multilevel marketing companies operate today.

The FTC did require some changes to our pricing policies, and required us to start providing each new distributor an eight-page explanation of our Sales Plan. They also reviewed our monthly distributor magazine and sales literature to ensure that no claims or photos represented wealth beyond what was realistic for most distributors to achieve. Amway still makes disclosures to make it clear this is a business that requires hard work and is not a "get rich quick" scheme.

Despite the ruling in our favor, the FTC's original misleading argument against us became a standard criticism in the years following for anyone who misunderstood our business or for former distributors who claimed they in some way were misled or that our business plan simply didn't work. Disgruntled former distributors and other critics were writing books that all pretty much made the same argument: they did not experience the success they were led to believe they could achieve.

As with the FTC, they apparently were not hearing the part about how the opportunity also requires work on distributors' parts. As the FTC found, the AMWAY Sales Plan makes clear the idea that work will be involved and that material rewards depend on the amount and quality of work. To our critics, we also pointed out that no one takes a financial risk from trying Amway. The only cost to distributors to start their own Amway business is a registration fee that provides them with literature, sales aids, and other support. Even if they decide to do nothing, they can use any products they purchase, which are backed with a satisfaction guarantee. We even refund the registration fee if new distributors decide the business is not right for them. If they try and fail for whatever reason, as the former distributors who testified in the FTC case admitted, they likely will be better off for having gotten involved with positive people in setting goals and making the attempt to build something for themselves.

Looking back at this case and similar criticisms of Amway, I have to admit I don't truly understand people who try to lift themselves up by tearing other people down or people who try to blame their failures on external forces instead of accepting responsibility for their lives. Many people have tried to build Amway businesses and failed. But if they are honest with themselves, they will admit that they didn't make the necessary effort to sell products and sponsor people.

Building your own business takes hard work, long hours, perseverance among setbacks, and maintaining a positive attitude. People who don't possess or want to accept these traits should seek other ways to make a living. I have nothing against someone who tries Amway and concludes the business is not for them. But I wish they would take responsibility for their own actions instead of trying to blame the business. If the Amway business is not sound, it could never have grown and prospered for more than half a century. Perhaps those who testified against Amway in the FTC case were looking for some form of compensation or satisfaction. But I don't think a judge or any settlement could have provided them what they truly needed.

Many years after Amway started to succeed, some people were saying they lamented the fact that they had had a chance to invest in the early days and get in on the ground floor. This must be wishful thinking, because we never offered a partnership or ownership share in Amway. If anyone in the early days or up to this day wants to build a successful Amway business, they need not and cannot invest in the company. All they need to do is sign up, pay a few dollars for a sales kit, and diligently work the plan with an eye toward never giving up until they achieve their goal.

The Amway opportunity provides the same potential for success today as at the start of the business in 1959. Amway was a ground-floor opportunity in 1959 and remains so today for anyone who wants to sign up as a distributor and is willing to focus, work hard, and persevere to achieve a dream.

In the end, the FTC case proved to be helpful in proving our legitimacy, especially as we expanded overseas—even though we considered the suit another government misunderstanding of business principles and an attack on free enterprise. Fortunately, the drawn-out investigation and the publicity surrounding it did not hurt our growth. Just four years after the FTC brought the suit, our reported sales at retail more than tripled—to $800 million.

Unfortunately, that was not the case with the next major challenge we had to overcome. In 1982, the Royal Canadian Mounted Police raided our headquarters in Canada and claimed in a statement to the press that Amway had defrauded Revenue Canada, the country's equivalent to our Internal Revenue Service, of an undetermined sum in excess of $28 million CAD in customs duties. With penalties, it sought $118 million USD. Revenue Canada threatened Jay and me with extradition to stand trial in a Canadian court.

I thought the Canadian charges were totally uncalled for. Knowing what we know now, and looking back all these years later, that's probably pretty correct. As time went on, it became evident to me that they didn't like our promotion of free enterprise. Nonetheless, I lost sleep over the Canadian suit. The FTC case was an important issue, but it was a business issue, and we just had to argue that out with our government. The Canadian government, however, was charging us with fraud. We were threatened with a serious jail term. That got my attention. People who know you don't think you're guilty. But that didn't mean it was the case for a lot of other people who didn't know us at all.

We had been operating in Canada under the terms of a 1965 tax agreement and had never before had problems with Canadian customs officials or Revenue Canada regarding the products we shipped or the amount of taxes we paid. Revenue Canada unilaterally changed the rules in 1980. We were a U.S. company shipping products across the border to a company we owned in Canada. We were selling products to our Canadian distributors, who were selling them at suggested retail to their customers.

Revenue Canada was suddenly disputing the taxable value of our products and the level of taxes we should be paying based on the value of our operations in Canada, so it became a complicated struggle. It felt political to me. Amway paid a fine of $21 million to end the criminal dispute. The civil battle dragged on for six long years until we finally decided to end the legal cost of fighting and pay a settlement of $38 million. That was about 40 percent of what the Canadian government claimed Amway owed and not a huge sum considering our reported annual sales for 1989 of $1.9 billion. But it was the largest contribution I ever made—without getting a building named after me.

As much as we hated to pay millions of dollars to settle a dispute in which we felt wrongly accused, the real damage from the Revenue Canada suit, and the reason we finally decided to settle, was the negative publicity that kept steadily dripping out and hurting our business. We could not continue to live with newspapers constantly pointing out that the punishment for fraud for which we were charged was jail terms up to twenty years. This was more than just a tax case. It set us back greatly. We had to reestablish our honesty. Both our Canadian and U.S. business dropped substantially. Our sales were down for several years before we could get going again. We lost some Canadian distributors but are grateful for the many who stuck with us and continued to build their businesses. Five years after the case was settled, newspaper articles still made references that we had been charged by the Canadian government with fraud. That's a word no one in business ever wants tied to their name.

If not for the publicity, we could have carried on with the lawsuit and seen it through. But you can't take being put in the news every time they decide to say something in Canada to remind everybody that you're being charged with fraud. The case seemed to be in the newspaper over and over. I was reluctant to visit our Amway Grand Plaza Hotel in downtown Grand Rapids at that time because of the feeling that people would have bad things to say. With such negative publicity, you just don't feel like you want to be seen in public.

The *Grand Rapids Press* put us on the front page every day. I got angry at the managing editor.

He told me sometime later, "You need to get used to the fact that you're front-page news." I was complaining at the time about a story that I considered not important enough to be on the front page, and I told him so.

He said, "If your name is involved, it's front-page news. Because everything you do is front-page news. Just accept the fact. You're a leading citizen of this town, so anything you do, good or bad, is going to be front page." And that's pretty well still true today.

Jay and I were consumed in those years with everything relative to this case. Much of our attention was focused on how to handle it, how the lawyers were moving on it, what actions to take, what defenses to make, interviews with the attorneys on building our case. We kept our airplanes out of Canada so they couldn't be confiscated. We closed our factory in Canada. We thought about just closing up Amway Canada, but we had too many distributors and employees depending on us.

Looking back, that showed our level of commitment to our distributors; we weren't going to walk away from them. But we couldn't afford to have our name blasted regularly on the front page of the newspaper. It was hard for distributors to sell and market in those conditions, but they had businesses that we needed to protect, and finally we felt we should settle. We also had to think of our families. In these situations, often the children also bear the brunt of accusations against their parents. I remember the kids expressing their concerns about the case at the dinner table and it being a major topic in our family prayers—including some tearful ones.

The Revenue Canada publicity also caught the attention of other major media that wanted to take a shot at us. We learned in 1982 that the popular Sunday-evening CBS News program *60 Minutes* was producing a segment on Amway and already had been filming large conventions sponsored by independent distributors. Especially after the stinging publicity over Revenue Canada, we had reason to be worried. The popular joke in those days went, "You know it's going to be a bad day when you arrive at your office and find Mike Wallace and a *60 Minutes* crew waiting for you."

Mike Wallace had a reputation for "ambush" interviews, so we made sure we were prepared. Since we knew *60 Minutes* was planning on doing a segment on Amway, instead of waiting for

Wallace to show up and catch us off guard we invited him to Amway and welcomed him and his crew. I think our offices and facilities blew him away. We were polite to them, and extended every courtesy to them that we would to any other visitor. I think that really set a positive tone, and we all thought his interview with Jay and me went fairly well. However, that's not to say we weren't experiencing some worry and stress as they completed their work on our story.

60 Minutes spent a year on its investigative segment, called "Soap and Hope," which aired on January 9, 1983. It included comments from disgruntled former distributors, footage of speakers at Amway conventions that were taken out of context and may not have best reflected *all* distributors, and tough questions about Canadian customs duties. But, overall, the general consensus was that the piece was balanced. If nothing else, viewers had a glimpse of a company much larger and more sophisticated than many expected, and they saw Jay and me being comfortable and forthcoming with Mike Wallace in explaining a company of which we were very proud.

Things actually ended on a positive note with Wallace. A year later we invited him to opening ceremonies for a new tower that had been added to a hotel that Jay and I bought and renovated—the Amway Grand Plaza (more about that later). *The Larry King Show* did a live radio remote broadcast in the lobby and King interviewed Wallace, who told King: "We thought we would have to do the story without cooperation, but these are classy people. They opened up to us a certain amount and took their lumps. We found their products are good, and they're not a pyramid operation." He even said in an interview with our local newspaper, "The people in Ada are first-rate." As I told distributors after the program aired, "We were first approached a long time ago. We tried to put it off, but they said they were going to do a show with or without us. And we finally took it upon ourselves to say that if they're going to do it anyway, we're not going to dodge it. Even if it's a disaster, we're at least going to stand for what we believe. We're not going to run from it."

Shortly after the *60 Minutes* piece aired, Jay and I were invited to go on the nationally syndicated *Phil Donahue Show*. Phil Donahue made his reputation by covering controversial subjects and giving his audience members the chance to ask questions of his talk-show guests. We learned in advance that the show had put together an audience of disgruntled distributors.

Jay said, "I'm not going on that show. I'm not going to acknowledge them. Let them have their show, but I'm not going to be there."

I said, "I am. I'm not going to have them announce that we were asked to come but neither one of us was willing to show up. I'd rather screw up than be absent and not able to speak for our position. I'll go."

I spoke in advance with Donahue, who explained that he would invite me to sit onstage with him, and we would take questions from the audience. I said, "Why do you have a show if people don't even know what we're talking about? Suddenly you have these people complaining about Amway without any context for the viewers." He said he would include an introduction to the show, explain the issues, and then we'd listen to distributor comments and questions. Even some complaints. After that, he would interview me based on audience comments.

When I arrived at his studio in Chicago, he said, "I've changed my mind. I'm not going to do an introduction; we're just going to start." So I ended up sitting on the edge of his stage, not onstage, in front of an audience of distributors, and Donahue turned them loose on me. Some were supportive and respectful, but many were combative. This was a down time for our business, so we had some distributors who weren't doing very well. Others were overselling the opportunity.

I tried to remain friendly, because I didn't want to get nasty against our own Amway people. I guess Donahue thought airing complaints would make Amway look bad. Because at the last minute he refused to open the show with any kind of introduction that would have provided context, viewers had no idea what was going on. Despite the mix-up, I think I held my own. Later that week I got a postcard from First Lady Barbara Bush with the message: "DeVos 10, Donahue 0." Through my years of supporting the Republican Party and candidates, I had gotten to be friends with President and Mrs. Bush, and her note was typical of her kindness.

In the end, the heightened attention from news media actually was beneficial in helping us see ourselves as others see us. That's when we started to zero in on making some changes by addressing the isolated incidents that contributed to misperceptions. We formalized rules and standards for the speeches and other materials distributors use for the Amway business, and we often have a corporate representative at distributor conventions. Distributors are only authorized to use product and business claims that are consistent with our standards. We are keeping abreast of what is being said and being claimed by our distributors, recognizing they are Amway in the public eye.

All of these government and media experiences, mostly negative, became just some of the challenges we had to overcome for the survival of Amway. The challenges were much larger and more serious than in the past, but the lesson is the same: keep trying instead of crying, persevere, and keep hope alive. Some of our earlier challenges seemed large—an unfinished airport when we were trying to get an aviation business started; our sailboat sinking in a deep, dark ocean; only two people showing up for a Nutrilite meeting. These were then dwarfed by our aerosol plant burning down. But even that disaster couldn't begin to compare to the threats from the FTC and Revenue Canada.

By the time Mike Wallace arrived at our door, we didn't have to accept that it would be a bad day. We knew that for anyone who dreams, dares to be different, or tries something new, the critics will always weigh in. In the early days we wanted Amway to become a household name. Later, when the Amway name also was used as a punch line to get cheap laughs on TV sitcoms, we simply accepted it as part of our growing fame and kept moving on to greater success. Anyone who rises high enough above the crowd will sooner or later draw the attention of critics. We weathered the storms and moved on.

By this time, we could consider challenges as just more obstacles to overcome, to go under, over, or around. This made us even better prepared for the next major chapter in our growing business. We were heading to the corners of the globe. At the time we may have thought it even too much of a challenge to consider, but soon the American way would be embraced in some of the most unlikely places in the world.

CHAPTER EIGHT

Exporting the American Way Worldwide

J AY AND I HAVE often been credited for being men of vision. But if that were true, we might have foreseen when we started Amway in 1959 that the desire to own a business was not limited to the American way. That may still have seemed true when we crossed the border to open for business in Canada in 1962—when we opened our first overseas affiliate, in Australia, nearly a decade later, we still had the mind-set of operating in a country with ideals very similar to those in America. But soon thereafter, with the opening of each new international market, the concept was clear: people around the world share a desire for an opportunity to have a business of their own. Seeing the AMWAY logo on signs accompanied by Japanese or Chinese characters was a bit of a jolt to me—a guy who once served overseas in a war to defend American democracy and came home eager to prosper within the blessings of freedom I'd felt only were available in our country. Today, we know differently. The dream of what we described as the American way cannot be contained within borders or limited by nationality.

We decided to go into Canada as our first international attempt. Jay and I were naïve at the time, thinking that in an English-speaking country we would not have to reprint our U.S. literature. We forgot that there are a lot of French-speaking people in Canada—which required us to print separate literature and product labels in French. We originally intended to open in Canada as a separate company contained within the Canadian borders and with no cross-border sponsoring, but it soon became obvious that starting all over was a bigger job than we were prepared to deal with. We concluded that we had a lot of people in the United States with connections in Canada and that we simply needed to figure out a way that where Amway grows, distributors grow; where we go, they go. Future overseas affiliates were started as brand-new companies, but we also developed a system allowing distributors to sponsor in all of our markets.

We opened in Canada within three years of starting Amway because distributors in the United States had friends, relatives, and business contacts there and wanted to take advantage of new markets. Ada is only about 150 miles from the Michigan border with Ontario. Except for Quebec, there was no language barrier, and Canada's economic and government structures and culture were very similar to ours. So it was easy for Amway to quickly take advantage of an expansion opportunity and become an international company. In comparison, our next international move was a giant step—an overseas market halfway around the world in Australia. The joke at the time was that by us choosing such a distant country, no one back home would ever discover if our first overseas venture failed. That, of course, was not true, and it also was not fully true that we chose Australia because of the same commonalities we shared with Canada.

The truth was that we really didn't choose Australia as much as Australia chose us. A common practice among Australians was registering the names of U.S. companies that they figured might one day open in their country. They would register the name, produce a few products with related names, and wait for the day when a U.S. company decided to open in their market. Because Australians then owned the registered trademarks, foreign companies needed to buy their names back to do business in Australia. That's what happened to us. An Aussie registered the name AMWAY in his country and even some other product names. He was a direct seller and was even selling cosmetics under our ARTISTRY brand name, which he registered for exclusive use in Australia. Our Australian attorney told us this was a routine situation there. He even had a form letter for a signature of agreement to buy trade names back. He told me all I had to do was travel to Australia, settle on a price with this individual, and get his signature of agreement on the letter.

Because I happened to be in Australia at the time, I set up a meeting with him. He was a nice enough guy, and we had a cordial chat. I told him, "I've got the paper here to sign; all we have to do is arrive at a number. You and I both knew we'd come here someday, and now is the day of reckoning, the day you were waiting for. So here I am." We negotiated, arrived at a reasonable number, I wrote him a check, and he signed the paper the lawyer had given me. After the negotiations, the guy who registered our names asked if he could become our first distributor in Australia. He'd been in direct selling and had some other good distributors under him, so we honored his request. With his established direct sales business, he actually helped us get off to a good start.

We thought Aussies might object to the name AMWAY because it was American. We found just the opposite to be true. They loved the "American" idea; they loved that the products came from America. We tried to manufacture in Australia, but found that Australians were much happier to have our products made in Ada.

Our international expansion in the early days really took off because distributors encouraged us to open markets in countries where they had connections. We were constantly hearing from distributors, "When are we going to open up in this country or that country?" They couldn't operate in any country until we first established our operations there, properly imported products, had printed literature, registered trademarks, and followed the country's regulations.

In 1973, we opened in the United Kingdom, another country with the same language and similar political and economic systems; and in 1974, Hong Kong, which at that time was under British rule. We opened in Germany in 1975, which was the start of a decade of international expansion across Europe. In 1979 we opened in Japan, which had been greatly influenced by America since the war.

It's a bit hard today to imagine Jay and me simply picking up and moving all over the world. As young men, I remember us being so isolated in America. When World War II started, sales of world maps increased rapidly as Americans reading about battles in far-off places wanted to locate the unfamiliar countries and cities they were reading and hearing about in the news. It's true that I traveled to the South Pacific during the war, and Jay and I later traveled all throughout South America, so by the time Amway started expanding internationally, Jay and I at least were somewhat sophisticated about the world. I can see now how all life experiences can be lessons for success that may not be immediately realized. This was still an era when international business was not the norm, so I'm proud that Jay and I took these early and rather bold steps toward international expansion.

We were in about a dozen international countries by the early 1980s, and our international expansion was based mostly on going where distributors saw potential from their relationships and on distributors sponsoring across borders to build their own international businesses. In the mid-1980s we started to look at international expansion more strategically and opening markets in countries with more diverse cultures and economies. We formed a department specifically for operating international markets, and my oldest son, Dick, was appointed to head this new division. Like the other DeVos and Van Andel children, Dick had completed a training program to learn every aspect of the Amway business, and he had had ten years of experience in various management positions. When Dick became vice president of international operations in 1984, international sales accounted for about 5 percent of all our business. When he left that position six years later, more than half of our sales came from overseas.

Dick really pioneered a strategic program of international growth and expansion after Jay and I got our international business off the ground. Once Dick was in charge, opening international markets shifted from reacting to distributors who had friends in other countries to becoming a planned entry. His department for international expansion had a staff committed solely to opening new markets. They had all the expertise required to move to a country and plan and execute all the legal, regulatory, government, translation, logistics, advertising, and marketing necessary to open a market and begin holding meetings for interested potential distributors.

Those opening meetings were usually large, with sometimes as many as five thousand people showing up. We could never really predict how many people would reply to an invitation to an open meeting to explore the Amway business. I once said to Jay,

"Everybody knows somebody somewhere, and they can try to recruit them." That proved to be true. Distributors would travel from around the world to the new market openings and bring people they knew in those new markets to their first meetings. International sponsorship became a way for many of them to quickly grow their businesses.

Dick had a strategic plan based on ranking countries, from those that would be the easiest to open to the difficult countries that might pose the greatest challenges and risks. He helped us think even bigger by teaching us that we could maintain our core business principles while adapting our business model to more varied local customs, traditions, and legal and fiscal requirements, and really deserves the credit for our global success today.

China, at the time, was a big risk. The Chinese government required us to manufacture our products in their country, which required building a manufacturing plant and operating in a new way. After we opened, they outlawed multilevel marketing because of fears of possible abuses that were, though unfounded, a concern in a country that was in the early stages of accepting free enterprise principles. Eva Cheng, who was leading our market development in China, called me and said, "What are we going to do now?" I told her to let the Chinese government know that we intended to stay and abide by their rules. We had to open retail stores in China and invent new ways to reward distributors based on the size of their businesses. I believe the power of the Amway opportunity has strong appeal for people in China who are trying to build better lives more in line with what we enjoy in America—and that our way of business will one day be embraced by the Chinese.

Today, China is Amway's largest market, and our business there continues to grow.

But I marvel at the fact that Amway even operates today in China and Russia—once considered forever cut off from the free world by the Bamboo and Iron Curtains. Promoting our entrepreneurial way of business in these countries had been unthinkable just a few years prior.

I also think back to when I served on that tiny island in the Pacific when America was trying to defeat the empire of Japan, and how Japan is one of Amway's more successful affiliates today. Similarly, who could have imagined during the Vietnam War era that one day an American company based on capitalism and free enterprise would be thriving in Vietnam and building factories there? That may have sounded crazy not so long ago, but today Amway is thriving in the country of our former communist enemy.

During the 1990s, Jay and I had a new photo taken for use in distributor publications. To illustrate our stature as a global company, we had our portrait taken standing on either side of a large world globe. It's amazing today to see that portrait hanging in offices in China next to signs printed in Chinese characters, or to see the AMWAY logo displayed against the backdrop of a skyline in Shanghai.

In an article about our growing business in Japan in 1990, *Forbes* magazine interviewed an accountant who had become a distributor. "Amway's be-your-own-boss pitch may be greeted cynically in the U.S.," he said, "but in regimented Japan, it finds a willing audience, especially among housewives and frustrated salarymen. There is little chance for success here, but with Amway, I see people succeeding all the time." We talk a lot in Amway about dreams—never giving up on dreams, not letting others steal your dreams. Now many Japanese can share with Amway distributors worldwide in dreaming of better lives.

Today my encouraging phrase "You can do it" has become a slogan repeated around the world in the Amway business. In Japan or China, you can hear distributors cheering and saying, "You can do it!" They ask me to sign their books with "You can do it!" It's become a rallying cry in Asia. That positive phrase has been carried around the world to people who often have likely been told they cannot do much of anything.

When Amway opened in Russia, I was asked to call from my home in Florida and tell a meeting of about six hundred people, "You can do it!" Our people over there told me it was the most raucous meeting they ever had. These Russian people were excited by the idea of being free to have their own businesses and doing something of substance for themselves. I was told people were standing on the chairs, singing and cheering—an atmosphere more like a football game than a sales meeting!

Of course, entering countries with different languages, cultures, and governments did not make our job easy and was not without its challenges. We were often the first direct-selling company in some Asian markets, where we faced tax, legal, and regulatory uncertainties. Our business in China had starts and stops while the government ruled on the legality of our style of business. In the end, we were able to keep operating, but unlike in other markets, we had to adjust our operations by selling products in retail stores.

The South Korean government was very suspicious of direct selling and thought our imports contributed to their trade deficit. But we demonstrated to the South Koreans how Amway could be a positive force in their country, and today we are a welcome business. I'm still amazed to look at photos of an arena filled with many thousands of South Korean distributors listening to me speak and knowing they all are attending because they are excited about the opportunity to own a business. We also proved in India and Thailand that our business was adaptable by establishing retail centers. It's incredible to visit Thailand, India, and China today and see modern, gleaming Amway buildings with our corporate and product logos prominently displayed to passersby.

As someone who lived through the Cold War with the Soviet Union and is a longtime advocate of free enterprise, I was thrilled and heartened when we started opening markets in the former Soviet bloc countries of Eastern Europe in the 1990s. We set up product centers, and many people in these countries—where such home and personal care products were scarce—stood in line to buy everything we offered.

In Hungary, we had eighty-five thousand distributors within the first year. I remember visiting these countries in those days, and they were rather bleak, gray places with grim-faced people who had few of the material possessions and opportunities that we take for granted in America. Bringing our opportunity and products to these people helped breathe a little new life and hope into this part of the world that for so many years longed for freedom.

In the 1990s we also opened a market in Brazil, which led to future expansion into many other South American countries as well. Jay and I were nostalgic over this—how could we ever have known, when we were traveling through South America as young men after our sailboat sank, that one day we would own an international corporation that would be formulating beauty products especially for the preferences of Latinos?

Whether people live in the Far East communist country of China, south of the equator in the emerging country of Guatemala, or in the established democratic South Pacific country of Australia, our experience has been that people around the world share one thing in common: they all dream of better lives. As reported in the Amway 2011 *Global Citizenship Report:* "Believe in Better." I'm heartened that Amway continues not only to do well in the world but to do good in helping people move from where they are to where they want to be by building better lives for themselves and their families, as well as for their communities and countries.

The Amway One by One Campaign for Children has raised more than $190 million and helped more than ten million children since the program began in 2003. In 2012 alone, Amway distributors and employees logged more than two hundred thousand volunteer hours for charitable organizations all over the world. Besides helping people, we also are helping our planet. In our tradition of environmental responsibility, we are helping to reduce our carbon footprint, conserve water, produce less waste, and protect habitats in each country where we operate.

This is not to brag but to make the point that I'm proud of our philosophy. Part of Jay's and my legacy is our belief in people prospering through their own efforts and talents, and spreading that belief by helping other people to help themselves. It's gratifying to see that this is a universal philosophy that produces such powerful results. This is another reason I've always been such an optimist, rarely seeing anything but the good in all people I meet.

———

BACK IN THE 1980s, when most of our business was still in the United States, we thought of Amway as being headquartered in Ada, Michigan. But as we began to hire new international employees, they told us, "Ada is not the center of the Amway world, even though you guys still think it is. Amway's center is all over the world. If you want to talk about where the real center is, it's in China. Because that's our biggest market." They were showing us how we still were looking at the business as U.S.-centered, and not getting our minds around the size of the business. We kept trying to bring everything back to Ada—for many years we tried to produce everything in Ada, at great cost and inconvenience, shipping things across the world, simply to make products and to provide jobs in Ada. Now we're building a plant in India, opening a new headquarters in Thailand, and building a second new plant in China. We have several major construction projects under way worldwide. People who come to Ada now cannot begin to grasp what Amway is, because it's not just in Ada anymore.

That retreat back in Charlevoix, Michigan, when we named our first board the American Way Association, seems a bit quaint now. In the early years of Amway, we were telling distributors to dream big, but we still had little idea of what dreaming big truly meant or could achieve.

The world has shrunk quite a bit since then. Strangers across borders that once seemed firmer and in lands that once seemed farther away are today much closer and more familiar. We continue to translate our packaging and sales literature into scores of different languages, formulate products to appeal to specific tastes in different countries, and adapt to different regulations and cultures. But wherever we go in the world today, we continue to be reminded that all the world's people hunger for freedom and an opportunity to succeed through their own talents and efforts.

Our simple message of a business opportunity for all has become an international language. When I go onstage at a convention anywhere in the world the people in the audience might look different, but the enthusiastic reception is the same. It's difficult at times to fully connect that first little company in the village of Ada more than fifty years ago to the millions of Amway distributors around the world today.

I believe Jay and I were blessed for a reason: to found Amway on principles that would benefit all these people of the world. Our employees knew it before we did. Ada is not the center of the Amway world. The center of Amway is all around the world. And, I would add, the heart of the Amway opportunity is there, too.

CHAPTER NINE

Finding My Voice

I WAS INSPIRED BY MOTIVATIONAL speakers when I was first starting in business, and so I have strived to inspire thousands of
Amway distributors to stand in front of their own groups and
motivate them to keep going and keep growing. Encouraging others, cheering them on, telling them, "You can do it!" has become
an essential ingredient in what makes Amway what it is today.

Shortly after Jay and I started our flying school, we took a
Dale Carnegie course. We both felt that as young businessmen
and salesmen it was important for us to learn how to speak and

municate effectively. It turned out to be a very good experience for us, particularly for me, because it gave me new confidence as a speaker. The instructors were very skilled at pointing out areas for improvement without being critical, and they maintained a positive atmosphere that encouraged each student.

They taught me that the key to public speaking is to use illustrations. Tell stories, preferably from your own experiences. If you talk about something that happened in your own life, you don't need notes, because you lived it. So stories from personal experience are usually the best.

The Carnegie method also taught a speech formula. First, make sure you always tell your audience the subject of your speech. I've heard too many speakers talk but never tell me what they were really talking about. They talked about a lot of things, but I wanted to know, "What is the subject today? What are we going to be talking about? What's the point of this?" Second, tell the audience why we're going to talk about the subject. Why is the topic important? And third, illustrate the point of the speech. Illustrate, illustrate, illustrate!

After that, all that's needed is an opening—a joke or a greeting—and the close, which is nothing more than "Now that you've learned all I've told you, I suggest you take the following action." And those were the basics I learned in the Dale Carnegie class. I actually took the class again a few years later and was even more convinced of the power of illustrations.

Shortly thereafter, I was invited to speak to about three thousand people at a Nutrilite convention in Chicago. I followed the

Carnegie course and had the illustration part down. My subject was "white heat"—if you're going to succeed you've got to be intense and hot and on fire about what you're doing. At the close of my speech, I sat down, but everybody else stood up and gave me extended applause. My former Dale Carnegie instructor was in the audience and came running up to compliment me. That was the day I discovered I had a talent for speaking, so I kept following the formula and kept giving speeches.

Shortly after we started Amway, the woman who ran our bookkeeping department said to me, "We have a local association of bookkeepers here in town. I've heard you speak and wonder if you'd speak to our little group?" This was the first time anybody had asked me to speak outside of Amway and Nutrilite meetings, so I said I would be happy to speak to her group. When I asked her what she wanted me to talk about she had no suggestions. So I said, "I'll tell you what—I'm going to talk about America and the positive aspects of our country. There's too much negativity in the air right now." I wanted to give a speech about how wonderful this country is.

That was the beginning of my best-known speech: "Selling America." I started thinking about what I would say to this small group and just began jotting down all the positive things that had been happening during the early growth of our business. The more I delivered "Selling America," the more people responded. I delivered "Selling America" to thousands across the country. This speech was taped at a Future Farmers of America convention in Indianapolis and later pressed into a record that was sold as an album in the early 1960s. The recording then earned an Alexander Hamilton Award for Economic Education from the Freedoms Foundation.

"Selling America" was really the beginning of my public speaking career and my first speech that appealed to audiences outside Amway or Nutrilite. I received a growing number of speaking requests and spoke at many high school and college commencements, as well as to business clubs and others. We considered these speeches as a good promotion for Amway in the early days. I kept coming up with new speeches, mostly for Amway meetings, but ones that also had messages for general audiences. Some of those speeches—"The Three A's: Action, Attitude, and Atmosphere" and "The Four Stages"—I've given to Amway audiences worldwide. They're just good, fundamental talks.

I once even shared "The Four Stages" with President Gerald Ford. The speech covers four stages in the development of any organization: building, management, defending, and blaming. I had known Gerald Ford since he was our U.S. congressman from Grand Rapids. I was visiting him in the Oval Office one day, and was told I would have ten minutes to spend chatting with him.

During our chat I said, "You know, this whole town is in stage four."

He said, "What do you mean stage four?"

I said, "Well, stage four is a blaming stage, when everybody blames everybody else for the problems. That sounds like this town."

President Ford said, "That sure sounds like it to me, but tell me the rest of it."

I said, "I don't have any more time. They gave me ten minutes, and I must honor that."

He said, "I'd like to hear the rest of this."

So now I can say I once delivered my "Four Stages" speech to a prestigious audience of one—the president of the United States. And he was very positive about it, agreeing that we had to get this country back to stage one and think about building it rather than arguing about who gets credit or blame.

Sharing a speech with a U.S. president or recording a speech for a national audience was the exception. Most of my speeches, especially in the early days, were intended simply to motivate and encourage Amway distributors. One of my earliest for this purpose was "Try or Cry." I wanted to tell my audience, "You've got a choice in this business: you can cry or try." I told them stories about all the things Jay and I tried in starting and building our businesses. Some worked and some didn't. But the difference was, we kept trying. It was a simple speech, but it's still a good speech, and some people tell me they still listen to it on tape.

I've gained a reputation for speaking without notes. I may pull a piece of paper from my coat pocket on which I've jotted a few points, but these notes are simply a reminder of my subject and a list of stories I plan to tell to illustrate my point. I stick to the simple Dale Carnegie formula, and since I use stories from my life I can tell them from memory. When I first delivered "Try or Cry," for example, the speech was just pure memory. I'd lived all the things I talked about in that speech and I simply started talking to my audience: "Let me just talk to you tonight about what we've been through to get here."

I didn't need to be an expert in any field to be an effective speaker, but sometimes expertise in a specific area can lead to a good speech. I used my experience as a sailor to come up with my "Four Winds" speech. Talking about the winds and where they come from and how they affect us is something people can hang on to. So, long after the details of the speech may be forgotten, people still remember the illustrations of the "Four Winds" and what they can do.

I can easily repeat that speech because all I have to do is think of the winds I've encountered while sailing. It begins negatively with, obviously, a north wind. When people say why they can't succeed, or complain about conditions not being in their favor, it's as if they're fighting the cold north wind that can blow into our lives and shut us down for a while. An east wind can be a portent of bad weather ahead. In business we may face uncertainties that we must deal with, but it helps to look ahead and be prepared—just as when in life we see a dark sky and prepare with a jacket and an umbrella. But beware of the south wind—it's a fooler. It can lull you into thinking you're doing pretty well, and you feel content with the way things are going and let your guard down. You stop being aggressive. Business lags, and it's time to look for the west wind. West winds are the best kind, with settled weather and friendly breezes. With this wind behind us we can make great strides and cover long distances in a short time. This is the time you do a constructive review of your business, recruit energetically, and grow.

The audience could picture a sailboat as they were listening, and almost feel the effect of the winds; they would put themselves and their business into the picture and assess which wind they were encountering. Over the years, this speech has become a favorite of the distributors.

Of course, with Amway expansion around the world I discovered I needed to change my approach a bit when speaking to international audiences through a translator. The process becomes much more difficult. One of the first lessons I learned: don't tell jokes. They don't translate well. The first time I tried to use a joke in China I got no reaction from the audience. The same joke that usually got a laugh from English-speaking audiences resulted in dead silence from the Chinese.

While speaking in foreign countries I also avoid anything related to politics, because I'm not in my own country, and I'm not authorized by Amway to express my opinions. So I find something else to talk about.

In China, I once talked about overcoming objections to the Amway business and suggested how objections—also known as rejections—could be handled, since both in life and in selling we can experience rejection. To illustrate, I used my heart transplant. I was 71, and my medical records had been sent to some thirty doctors and transplantation centers; I was rejected by every single one. But one doctor in the whole world said yes. Although my odds weren't very good, we stuck with it until I found that *one* person, so I do know about rejection. In business we can also face long odds at times, but when you find that *one* person, your business—and in my case, my life—continues. Once I even held up the pills I've taken since receiving my new heart to prevent its rejection by the rest of my body. I told my audience, "I'm sorry I don't have any antirejection pills for *you,* to help you overcome the rejections you get in your business. You just have to keep on keeping on until you find—as I did—that *one* person who shares your vision and says yes.

Looking back at some of my speeches, I can be a bit more analytical about how they helped describe why Amway has succeeded and what the Amway business really is all about. I believe they helped distributors understand the essence of who they are as business owners and that they have a purpose and calling higher than simply selling products and building wealth. Yes, encouragement and motivation were essential in my speeches. But I've also realized that I had to speak to help define our business and clarify our true mission.

————

AMWAY IS IN THE business of helping other people. We have ART-ISTRY cosmetics, NUTRILITE supplements, and all the other products, and this is how people make money in the Amway business. But the real magic of the business is in helping people have better and richer lives. That's always been our focus. Amway distributors happen to sell products to get somewhere, but we're clear about where we're going. Amway started with the idea that anyone could have their own business. Jay's and my goal was to have a business of our own, and we thought everybody in the world wanted that. We still think that's a fundamental driver. People are oftentimes shocked when I say, "Distributors can sell their Amway business, they can pass it on to their family—it's an asset, a business they own and run."

Amway always has been about enriching the lives of others, by giving them better products and a whole new way to market them. After the Federal Trade Commission ruling, one of the judges said to me, "Amway is the first thing I've seen come along since supermarkets that was really a whole new method that had new potential for marketing. It's the only new thing I've ever seen beyond stores." The old door-to-door salesman goes back a long way, to my grandfathers and beyond. But this multilevel thing was totally new, and as we look back at it today we realize more now than when we started that it is one of the few opportunities in the world where people can start with next to nothing and build substantial incomes.

When Amway was first becoming successful, we were approached by W. R. Grace & Company, which included a large chemical company, an airline business, and a big shipping company. They were looking for a way to diversify and expand their company and were considering our type of business and thought they might buy Amway. We were just a nice little soap company with some home products in those days. A couple of Grace executives asked to talk to us about our company and the possibility of acquiring Amway. Jay and I weren't interested in selling but decided to listen to what they had to say—maybe just for fun to get a sense of what our company was worth to a potential buyer. They made an offer, but we told them Amway was not for sale. They said they still planned to expand, had a manufacturing plant to make our type of products in Cincinnati, and already had their Grace Home Products company set up.

"If you don't want to sell," we were told, "we're going to activate Grace Home Products and compete with you."

And that's when I said to him, "Terrific! If you're going to do it, do it right. I'll give you an Amway sales kit. It includes the whole Sales Plan. It's all outlined in there, and if you follow that you'll probably do okay. Because if you do it, I want you to do it right."

They did start Grace Home Products, but I never paid attention to it. A few years later, at an airport in Bar Harbor, Maine, I crossed paths with Peter Grace. I'd never met him, but I recognized him and introduced myself as one of the owners of Amway. I said, "How's your Grace Home Products company going?"

He said, "You know damn well."

I told him I really didn't because I hadn't followed the company. When he told me they closed the new venture, I said, "I don't understand. I gave you guys a book to follow and an Amway sales kit. Everything was in there. All you had to do was follow it."

He reached over and poked me in the chest and said, "Young man, you left something out!"

After relating that story in a speech in Las Vegas celebrating

Amway's fiftieth anniversary, I went on to tell the audience of distributors, "Today, I want to tell you what we left out of the kit. And if you ever leave it out of your kit or out of your business, your business will fail, and this whole business will fail. What Peter Grace thought was left out of the kit, we could never have put into one. It was an attitude of helping the people you brought in, so they in turn could help others. By helping others, you win.

"It's pretty old-fashioned, but that's just the way this business is run."

We understand that Amway is really in the business of enriching lives. One of my most popular speeches is "Life Enrichers," which I began giving in 1989 after I was struck by something that had been written by Walt Disney. I was on a plane to California, thinking I should come up with a new speech, when I came across this Disney quote. He wrote that there are three types of people in the world: "well-poisoners," who always criticize the efforts and ideas of others; "lawn-mowers," who are good citizens who go to work, pay their taxes, and maintain their homes but never venture beyond their own yards to help others; and "life-enhancers," who reach out to enrich the lives of others through helpful deeds or encouraging words. And I thought, "Wow! That type of person applies to Amway." I preferred the term *life enrichers* for my speech but based my talk on Disney's example and always gave him credit.

I'm still struck today by how being a life enricher is at the heart of Amway. Product sales are important, but the real importance is that by selling products, people make extra money to help improve their lives, and also have the opportunity to improve the life of somebody else by sponsoring them into the business, and they in turn sell products and bring others into the business, and the lives of all those people who want to do this kind of work are enriched. Their whole life changes, not only because people make some money selling our products, but also because they move into a new environment of positive people who think in terms of helping others to enrich their lives, too.

So, the whole concept of life enrichment is foundational to the Amway business. "Life Enrichers" was my major speech for a couple of years at Amway meetings, but I may actually have given it to just as many non-Amway audiences. I was excited about the concept of enriching lives and wanted to encourage as many people as possible with the idea that they could be life enrichers. To this day I send letters to people who are featured in our local newspapers for voluntary acts of kindness that I believe qualify them as life enrichers.

From the day I stood up at that Nutrilite convention in Chicago in the early 1950s and talked about white heat, through "Selling America," "Try or Cry," and all the other speeches I've given worldwide, I believe my speaking has played a vital role in not only helping Amway distributors achieve their dreams but in helping them appreciate the value of entrepreneurs and free enterprise and their responsibility to enrich lives. These speeches over the years were no less important to the success of Amway than developing products and building factories and managing the company. So many aspects go into a successful business. But nothing would have happened—especially in the early years of Amway—until we started to get people to believe in our business and in themselves. That effort, which was like a crusade in the early years, has reached people around the world. That kind of reach could only have been attained by people encouraging other people to join us so that they, too, could enrich their lives and those lives of their children, family, friends, and beyond.

Many times when I'm invited to speak I'll ask, "What would you like me to talk about?" And I often hear, "Oh, just encourage us, inspire us! We don't care. Give us one of your positive talks." People in business and life want to be, and need to be, encouraged and inspired. Such encouragement was a key to Amway's success, and I think any business or organization can be more successful if its leader is willing to stand up and deliver a positive message—from experience, from the heart, and, of course, with a lot of memorable illustrations.

CHAPTER TEN

A Magic Moment

I LOVE OWNING THE ORLANDO MAGIC—but I never set out to buy a basketball team, or for that matter any professional sports team. The opportunity came to me in a roundabout way.

Before buying the Magic in 1991, I was originally approached to be the owner of a potential new Major League Baseball team in Orlando. The majors at that time were seeking to expand the number of teams and had no teams in the rapidly growing state of Florida. But as it turned out, the National League decided to locate its new team, the Marlins, in Miami instead of Orlando. A few months after losing the bid for the baseball team, I learned that the owner of the Orlando Magic was interested in selling. Our family considered it, and although initially we really were more interested in baseball, we decided basketball might be a better choice. We spent winters in Florida, when basketball was played, and during the baseball season spent a lot of time in Michigan. As an indoor sport, we also thought basketball games would never have to be delayed or canceled due to bad weather.

So we ended up with a basketball team, and we've owned the team now for more than twenty years. Looking back at how much of my youth was spent shooting hoops and how I cheered for my high school basketball team, I must admit that my interest in owning the team was driven more by how much fun it could be than by any financial considerations. Professional sports ownership typically is not a very profitable business. The greatest advantage has been that our ownership is a family business that brings Helen and me together with our children and grandchildren in a common interest. Magic games have become a great bonding event for our family and a shared experience that crosses three generations. I'll never forget the first time our expansion team made the playoffs. The Magic was a new team, untested in playoff competition, and wasn't given much chance by the sports media. We didn't make it to the finals, but just being able to root for our team together, to keep hope alive that the Magic just might become the NBA championship team, was exciting and encouraging for our family.

I now realize and must admit that part of the fun for me is just knowing that this professional basketball team and organization is our family's. I get that boyhood thrill that business guys don't usually get. The kids love it, too. They take a genuine interest in how our team is doing and are integrally involved in the decisions that are being made to run it successfully. The Magic is often the center of conversation in our family when we get together. And we're excited that since our ownership the Magic has been in the playoffs about half the time. Our record of long-term performance is pretty good, and we've been blessed with some good draft picks, like Shaquille O'Neal and Dwight Howard.

One of my early lessons was how much an owner is expected to interact with the players. A problem with most new owners is that they haven't distinguished between their role and that of the coach. A lot of owners want to get in the locker room and be the coach. At first, I myself thought, "I guess I'll try to give the team a little 'pepper-upper' talk—they could use that right now." But I soon learned that was not my role; that's the coach's role. I'd overstepped my bounds a bit and had to learn not to stick my nose in too far. Early on, I would go into the locker room before the game, hang around for the team meeting, and give my little pep talk with the coach probably thinking, "We have a ball game to play. Why's this guy giving us attitude stuff when we're trying to remember a play?" Later, the coach mentioned something like this to me. As an owner, I had to learn my place.

My job was to hire the coach and let him be the coach. We all have different talents, and no one member of a team or any organization can play every role. I may have had the skills to lead and motivate Amway distributors and employees, but I had to admit I was not qualified to be a professional basketball coach!

Coaches make errors, but they need to make split-second decisions during the game. While you and I are enjoying the game the coach is trying to figure out what play to send in, which player to rotate in next, which player's performance is starting to decline because he needs to come out and rest, just to mention a few. A couple of times lately when we were losing a few games, I did call the coach to say I wanted to speak to reassure the team that the owners were still proud of them because I feel that sometimes players need to hear directly from the owners that we have faith in them.

I hope that as an owner I've had a positive influence on our players, particularly those who are in or barely beyond their teenage years when they suddenly become rich and famous. I may never know if my influence will have an impact, but I make the effort. Helen and I also try to have the team over to our house for dinner before the start of the season and I use this annual gathering as a special occasion to talk with them. Because more recently we've run up against scheduling challenges, we now go to Orlando and meet there for a meal—lunch or dinner, whichever works.

First of all, we have new players and maybe some new coaches each year, so I want them to know me and why I care about the team. I also want them to know about our faith. I want them to hear from me that their team's owners are Christians. If they have any questions, we can talk about it. I also take them through a little bit of our family history and share our reason for buying a team: to be a positive influence on players and help them have more successful and balanced lives.

Second, I talk to them about money and the importance of saving it. They're making a lot of money, but their time to earn is limited. As a pro basketball player, no matter your physical condition or how well you might take care of yourself, once you're over the age of forty, you're pretty much out of this business. Their bodies will eventually let them down. So if they want to live well the rest of their lives, they need to set themselves up financially for when that day comes. They're earning enough a year that they can afford to live, save, and invest—if they spend less than they make. I encourage them to realize that *now* is the time to save and invest and also to plan for charitable giving and set money aside for taxes. I also encourage them to hire an investment expert and have good financial counsel to take care of these things for them. Otherwise, they may wake up ten years later and say, "I wonder what happened to all that money?"

The third thing I discuss with the team is conduct. I read about players getting in trouble with drugs or alcohol or whatever, and their careers are ruined. I say, "You've probably been told a thousand times how quickly you can destroy your career. You're in a hot seat, you're a star, and there are always people who are going to attack you verbally or otherwise. Being an athlete and competitive, your instinct might be to fight back verbally or physically, and your career could be over in a moment. You hit somebody, you throw a bottle of beer, whatever, it's just an instant, but it's in the media. Maybe you go to jail or are arrested for drunk driving—all the talent and work you put into your NBA career is in jeopardy, just like that."

The players are polite and attentive when I go through this little litany. I tell them beforehand, "I've only got three points, so don't worry; it won't be a long preach."

We have conversations, and sometimes they talk and sometimes they don't. But I give my pitch anyway. I've owned the team long enough to at least know the things I think are important to players and that maybe will help them. They can choose whether they listen to an old guy trying to tell them what to do with their lives and money; but when they start missing their free throws and shots and their contract doesn't get renewed, and their money's been spent, I don't want them left wondering: "I was a big shot. What happened?"

I remember the first player we traded away was Scott Skiles. Helen felt so bad about it that she wrote Scottie a note saying in part, "I hope you can come back as a coach someday." She said to me, "We can't just let him go. He always gave a hundred and ten percent—I must write him a note." Of course, over many years in NBA basketball she realized it was not realistic to write a note to each player who left. But we still treat them with absolute respect, and I think that's why the Magic is rated one of the top NBA teams for ownership.

The Magic also has proven to be a tremendous public relations and marketing benefit for Amway. Games from the Amway Center are aired in more than two hundred countries. Who knows how many tens of millions of people are watching? Distributors can say, "This is our team." That's given a lot of our people a sense of ownership, that a founder of Amway owns that team.

———

YOU SIMPLY CANNOT OVERSTATE the power of being able to say something is "ours . . . I own it!" I've been thinking a lot lately about the importance of ownership. For many years, I served on the board of Grand Valley State University, which is near Grand Rapids, and have donated financially to this university. Our community has watched this institution, which started about fifty years ago as four small buildings on rural acreage, grow into two campuses with an enrollment nearing twenty-five thousand.

I was asked, "How did we get such a big crowd to come and support Grand Valley? There aren't that many people in this area who are alumni. So why is it that fifteen hundred people buy a ticket year after year to attend a fund-raiser that doesn't even feature an outside speaker but just includes tributes to local people who support Grand Valley?" I think part of the answer is that it's become *our* school—established in our community and grown with the help of local contributors. It was people within our own community who developed the concept for the new state college and, amazingly, sold the idea to the public of having a local university we could call our own.

Sometimes there is friction between a local college and the local community—tension over the fact that universities don't pay property taxes, that there may be incidents of student misconduct, or that taxpayers need to pay to provide added police or fire protection. But in our case we are proud to support Grand Valley State University and even claim it as "our school." I received an honorary doctorate from them once upon a time, so I claim Grand Valley as *my* school. But the concept of *our* school, *our* church, taking ownership of something that we are involved in, or respect needs to be a vital part of our culture.

When we think of Grand Rapids as *our* town, we feel differently, even drive differently; we pick up after ourselves more easily. And when it's your town, you welcome a stranger on the street. I say, "Welcome to Grand Rapids!" Because it's *my* town, *our* town. This whole concept of people being owners makes a huge difference.

It's the difference at Amway, in my opinion. Any of our distributors can say, "It's *my* business." The concept of *ours* is such a huge motivator that we must try to engage that power whenever we can. It's important to me that my children and grandchildren realize America is *their* country. My grandchildren say, "Grandpa is so proud of his country! He served in World War Two." I need them to appreciate that it's *their* country and *their* future.

I spoke recently about this concept of "ours." Maybe that's why I get such a kick out of being the owner of a team and being able to say "our team" and knowing that all the fans can say "our team," too. I'm proud to own a business and even more proud to know how many Amway distributors around the world today can say, "This is our business: we own it, we're invested in it, involved with it, make decisions about how to run it, and share its blessings with our family." That's why Helen and I have supported the development of downtown Grand Rapids. It's *our* town! We feel a responsibility for its quality of life and continued growth. I want to live in a community that is a life-enriching one. That's been my theme all my life.

I'm also so pleased that we've been able to have an impact on the Orlando community. We have the only big-league sports team in town. And Orlando has worked with us beautifully and helped us build an arena because they knew we needed a new building. So the town has been good to us, and we've tried to be good to Orlando. We and our players give to the community, including funding programs at the University of Central Florida, sponsoring youth athletic programs, and players visiting children in hospitals. I think the participation of our ballplayers with the area's young people gives those players a greater sense of value in themselves — as they build relationships with the kids, they build pride in themselves. And we're proud of them for participating.

For me the Magic is sort of a "why" question in my life. Why was I offered the opportunity to buy a basketball team, and why did I accept? Maybe it's because I'm in the position to help young men build better lives. Or maybe because I have the opportunity to have a positive influence in the Orlando community. Owning an NBA team has helped teach me, and remind me, of so many principles that I've found valuable in my life: the value of owner-ship, contributing to a community, sharing with family, mentor-ing young people, the joy of winning. Looking back more than two decades to when the chance to purchase a team was pre-sented, I can see I didn't realize that I was deciding to do so much more than just buy a basketball team.

PART THREE

LIFE ENRICHER

CHAPTER ELEVEN

Fame and Fortune

WE LIVE IN A society today that seems to be fascinated by fame and fortune. I cannot deny that I have achieved a fortune and a certain level of fame—but any wealth or notoriety I have gained was never my goal but simply an outcome of my lifelong work and my interest in continuing to build a unique opportunity.

I really have no idea of when I became a millionaire, probably because Jay and I put a lot of money back into the business—especially in the early years—and gave ourselves minimum incomes. But there does come a day when you wake up and say, "Wow! This company's worth a lot of money." It wasn't a feeling that I personally had a lot of money. I remember the time a local college president came to ask me for a donation. I remember saying to him, "I don't have that kind of money."

He said, "But you've got a big company."

"We do have a big company," I said, "but I personally don't have that kind of money to give away yet. That will come, but you see, right now we're putting a lot of money back into the company." We didn't take a lot of money out of the business for ourselves. It's like I tell my ballplayers: "You take that money and go have fun with it, and someday you're going to ask, 'What happened?'"

For Jay and me, our first responsibility to the company always was to meet the payroll. If there's any common failure in business, it's the failure to give employees their paychecks. Meeting the payroll is not a small responsibility in business: you need to have the money to pay your people.

When Jay and I would drive over the hill approaching Ada and look down at that big Amway complex of factories, offices, and warehouses, we'd say, "Isn't that something?" I asked Jay once, "How do you feel when you come over that hill?" He said, "I'm kind of awestruck, but I don't spend a lot of time staring in awe. I just try to figure out how we can make it bigger." That's what we always talked about: how do we make it bigger and better? The size and worth of the company at any given time was not important. The important questions were always: How can we make it bigger? How do we share this concept of hope and profitability with more people? How do we fire up the whole world and let people know how valuable each one is?

This is what the Amway business is all about—helping other people achieve and improve their lives. Faith, hope, recognition, and reward: that's what it is. Jay and I were brought up during the Great Depression and were in a war that kept us thinking about values and conduct. The ethical base of helping the other guy is sometimes hard to find these days. I think our society's ethical base has slipped quite a bit. "Who cares about the other guy? As long as I get mine, it's okay." We've avoided that attitude pretty well in our business. We kept our focus "on the other guy." Help the person you sponsor, and if he does well, you'll do well. It's a bottom-up business.

In the very early days, Jay and I would invite Amway distributors into our homes, which were next door to each other. Those houses would never be considered mansions, and compared to many homes today would look rather small and ordinary. But we were proud of the homes we built on nice pieces of wooded property on a hill overlooking a river. Being in our houses blew some distributors away, but it really didn't matter whether it was a big house or a modest one. What mattered was that we were the founders and we invited them into our homes. We were showing our appreciation to distributors, not trying to show off.

We never considered ourselves or presented ourselves as being wealthy or superior. We drove modest cars. Jay's dad sold Plymouth and DeSoto cars, so that's what we drove. I never owned a Cadillac until we were pretty far along in our business. We became millionaires because of our concern to help our distributors make money. We kept reinvesting in the company, so for a long time we had modest incomes. As I said, we were conservative about taking any money out of the business.

Thinking back, I realize that Jay and I were trying to be very sensitive to our responsibility to our employees and independent distributors. We had thousands of people depending on us. I couldn't imagine us failing in some way that would have put others at risk. That was a huge responsibility for two young men. Also, I don't think either one of us could deal with the possibility of Amway failing, because it was more than just a business to us. Amway was our idea, our pride and joy, the confirmation of our belief that free enterprise really works. We thought in terms of family and children and schools and saving—setting money aside and having a budget. We've always tithed, putting a set amount aside for charitable and church giving.

In our case, however, it got to the point where we could afford just about anything. So why don't I buy, say, a bigger house or boat or airplane than what I have? I ask myself those questions sometimes, and the answer may be yes, or it may be that I have no reason for it. Sometimes a bigger plane or house or boat won't do anything more for you. But you do arrive at a point where you must decide why to do or not do something. If we had extra money, we could also make other choices such as giving more to charity or committing more to saving or investing (which is a way of supporting the business ideas and success of others).

I regularly discussed money with my children when they were growing up, and we talked about some of the possible pitfalls that can come with wealth. They're adults now, and we still talk about it. They have all accepted the responsibilities of wealth well. When you have wealth you have a lot of options. When you're poor, you simply don't have many options—so when your kids ask for money, you say you don't have any. End of story. But in our case, when the kids came to us and said, "How about getting me a car?" we had to discuss why we should or should not help them buy a car, and ask the question whether it should be new or used. The option of "we can't afford it" wasn't available at all.

It's easy to spoil your children. But I frankly don't think mine are spoiled. Even though they have great wealth, I don't worry about them misusing the money. I realize that some children do not use family wealth wisely and make bad decisions. Perhaps that happens to those who receive money without a good understanding of how it was earned, or who may never have worked to earn an income, or were never expected to work for their money. All my children were expected to work (all of them chose to work in the Amway business for a while, too . . . from the plant and warehouse floors to the administrative offices). They learned the foundation of working in going to Amway and being a member of a department, learning the business. No pressure was put on them to work, they just knew work was an important part of life and were happy to go. We actually bought a summer home nearby so they could go to work back home in Ada when school was out. They drove to work each morning like many other kids earning money during the summer.

I also think this work ethic is being passed on magnificently well to our grandchildren through their exposure to our various family business interests by being members of our Family Assembly, which they may join at age sixteen. While they can't vote until they're twenty-five, they can start to participate, learn, and express their views. We have a defined process and treat them with respect, teach them responsibility, and help them understand the value of work.

When you achieve wealth you are forced to determine its value and how your money is going to be spent. When I first married Helen, she suggested that we set aside 10 percent of our income up front and not wait to see what was "left over" for giving. We've been able to do that and more. That money is now set aside in our foundation, which gives us a very clear way of planning our giving and having money set aside so that when we are asked to give an amount to an organization or project, we never have to take anything "out of our pocket," which I think has allowed us to give with an even more generous spirit.

And then of course one question always comes up: "Should I even have this much wealth in the first place?" I feel the Lord allocated some money for us to use for our pleasure, some for our ability to experience His world, some for investing to help create economic expansion and job opportunities for others—and, of course, some for sharing with those who have real need. It's not because we're better or we're entitled to more money; we have been entrusted with it, and therefore need to be especially responsible. We just make sure personal spending doesn't become a priority over the giving side. Once you learn the budgeting process of setting aside for giving *first*, then what you have left you can allocate elsewhere—including a home or an airplane or a boat. One could always argue that these things aren't necessary and that you could give away more, and that's always true. But if you look at it that way, you'd never do anything more than take the bus.

But if you have a *love affair* with money, then maybe you shouldn't have wealth at all.

Once I bought a big helicopter, and after some future consideration said, "I don't need this. It's too big and makes too much noise." I felt it was a bit of an overreach for me, and I felt guilty for spending too much on something I didn't really need or even want that much. So I sold it (and, oddly enough, made some money on it).

When you have almost unlimited wealth, you have to make decisions about doing something or not doing something in ways that most people never have to consider, so watch out for your ego, watch out for the desire just to "show off." I think I got it wrong with that big helicopter, so I fixed it. Yes, I still fly in private planes and helicopters today—but never at the expense of generous giving.

———

JUST AS I HAD to start deciding how to handle wealth, I also needed to learn to handle growing personal recognition. When

Amway's success as a company became more widely known and more outside groups were inviting me to speak, I was very grateful. We had been ridiculed and called a lot of things in the early days of our business. The medical profession especially had choice words for our selling vitamins; a few doctors had studied nutrition (minimally, as one doctor told me), but most doctors in that day had not yet taken vitamins and minerals seriously as aids to better health. We had been challenged by the Federal Trade Commission—called a pyramid scheme, among other things—and acceptance came gradually.

We eventually stopped hearing the bad things and started getting some decent press about what we were doing and how the lives of people were being changed. Even the original negativity of the Federal Trade Commission case turned out to be a positive by giving Amway legitimacy. Jay and I were appointed to a growing number of boards, and the people on these boards treated us with respect and listened to what we had to say. People in the business community were fascinated with our views.

I once gave my "Man's Material Welfare" speech at an event for Dow Chemical, which is located in Midland, Michigan. The speech explained how people use raw materials to create products that they then sell in a free-market economy and earn wealth. This huge international corporation was interested in promoting freedom and free enterprise, and the company used my speech as a teaching tool with its employees. Instead of simply dismissing Amway out of hand, people were starting to ask about us and learn about our business. As Amway started growing around the world, there was a gradual recognition and even amazement about what we were doing, and the message of greater opportunity for all with free enterprise in a free land was growing.

I don't know that the growing recognition of Amway and me as a cofounder made me feel any different. Jay and I were pretty happy in what we were doing and pleased that our business was growing and that more people were catching on to it. Being well-known means there's a mix of people out there—some who are interested in what you're doing and others who don't care. We found that the people who paid attention to Amway were often those who were interested in business—especially unique businesses. We'd been doing some things with our Sales Plan that surprised people with its success. No one thought that a business built around helping other people to help themselves could grow to this extent.

I've become used to our being headline news in Grand Rapids. I don't know when all of a sudden Jay and I were considered leading citizens, as important figures and contributors to the city—the recognition was probably as much for civic contributions as it was for the size of our business. With so many new buildings being named for Jay or me, our names were popping up in too many places to be ignored.

For years, as I traveled worldwide giving speeches to distributors, I always received rousing standing ovations, and I've been asked how all that adulation makes me feel. Standing backstage in an arena seating tens of thousands, listening to your glowing introduction, and then hearing thunderous applause as you step into the spotlight can be a very heady experience.

But I have tried to not let it go to my head. For one thing, I know I'm just a sinner saved by grace—not a rock star, even if some people may have treated me as one. I believe the response I feel in those moments has been one of gratitude. Many distributors in these audiences started with little and have built successful businesses through the Amway opportunity. They are showing their appreciation for that opportunity. We also have a long tradition in Amway of standing to welcome any speaker as a sign of respect and appropriate recognition. We stand up and applaud for a lot of people in our business, because we recognize that anyone speaking on our stage is an important person.

Of course, whenever I spoke to an organization outside Amway, I had a bit of a different attitude—a positive response was important and made me feel terrific. When I didn't get a standing ovation, I wondered if I'd done a good job. My speeches were always positive and pro-America, so I had to ask myself, "Is the positive response only because my message is different from what audiences are hearing most of the time?" They were hearing presidents and politicians and the news media talking about the problems of America and how bad things were. They wanted to hear some good news, especially about their country—so I delivered good news, and they responded enthusiastically.

As a result, Amway developed a culture of praise and recognition for doing a good job. We don't just say thank you followed by polite applause. We stand up and cheer. All sorts of people in every community deserve to be recognized—but how often are they cheered? In our business, we stand up and recognize people, and eagerly leap from our seats to applaud and show appreciation.

My vision with Jay was always to work hard and impact the world for good. Perhaps my books and speeches have affected people's lives; if so, I'm grateful. Our goal was that anyone who is interested has a chance to succeed. If we didn't even have a product to sell, it still would be a wonderful thing to have a society where people come to weekly meetings to be encouraged about how well their life, their company, or their country is doing. That positive attitude should be in everybody's life.

I think people have reacted positively to my speeches not only because of what I did building Amway, but because they have dreams that they can do it, too. People want desperately to be told they're okay, they're good, they're capable. My goal has been to not only assure them of that, but also offer them an opportunity to achieve their potential. In the end, people want to be told, "You can do it!" and I have been happy to tell them just that.

The first time you get your name in the newspaper, you clip it out because you're worried that you might never see it in there again. I remember the first time I had a speaking engagement other than to an Amway audience—my first little "Selling America" talk. I looked for some coverage in the newspaper, but I guess the speech wasn't significant enough yet for an article. As the years went by and I became more successful, the media started covering my speeches, which was very gratifying. And today Amway and I get a lot of publicity—the media generally likes what I do and what I say, and there are times when they disagree, and that's okay. Because I'm seen today as a community leader, when a news release is sent out about an event, the media typically shows up—I'd like to think that's in recognition that I've worked hard in my life to be a successful person and especially a person who tries to make a positive difference in the lives of others.

When my eldest grandson, Rick, was in high school, he complained to his parents that my name was on too many buildings and kids teased him about it. I told him, "Rick, in your case, you happened to be born into this family. We're a family of people who are successful in life and businesses that help others. Now that's pretty significant all by itself and worthy of recognition. And therefore, our name does get mentioned in the media and put on buildings. But that's partly because we helped pay for that building or were the driving force to raise the money to bring that building into being. So you don't have to be embarrassed about seeing the DeVos name around—you can be proud of it. I would treat it, Rick, as a blessing that you are in a family of people who do things that are worthy of being talked about."

I never heard him complain about it again. He's grown up to do some great things for a young man just out of his twenties, including starting the ArtPrize competition, an event that attracts thousands of artists from around the world to Grand Rapids and hundreds of thousands of spectators who view the art and vote for their favorite entries to win significant cash prizes. Now he's in the newspapers and even national magazines more than I ever was at that age, and I'm very proud of him.

Honoring people who have done things that are worthy of being covered by the media, or are applauded and receive a standing ovation, is something we need to cultivate. When my speeches are applauded, I take it as a sign of agreement with what I'm talking about, not as praise for me personally. Yes, it's a nice feeling to be cheered, but I don't let it go to my head. I know I need to earn respect every time I speak. We happened to be in a business that requires a cheerleader, so I became a cheerleader.

I'm a positive person. I see things in a positive light and always come out on the positive side of any issue. I've been accused of not being critical enough or not finding faults quickly enough, and that's undoubtedly true. I don't see faults much. I'm not good at seeing the bad side. It's just my nature to look for the good in people. I know in life you need to be a little more discerning and more critical, but that isn't my style. I think there's some good in everybody, and almost everybody's got something worthwhile to say. And perhaps, just perhaps, that attitude has been a key to making me both wealthy and well-known.

CHAPTER TWELVE

Family Riches

A FAMILY BUSINESS! THAT ALWAYS had a nice ring to it. "Family" is one of the official four foundations of the Amway business. In fact, most Amway distributors work together as husbands and wives and even involve their children in their businesses. Jay and I had always been proud to tell distributors that Amway was a family business. They could be confident that as the owners, we—not public stockholders—had the final say about how our business would be run. Because it was our own business, we had a serious stake in seeing Amway succeed both in the short term and the long run. Distributors also had the assurance that we would make sound business decisions based on our experience as successful entrepreneurs and that we would treat our employees and all our business associates fairly, based on our ethical Christian backgrounds and principles.

Today, I'm proud that Amway continues to be a family business. My youngest son, Doug, is the president, and Jay's oldest son, Steve, is the chairman. I'm gratified by how they work together in a fashion similar to that of Jay and me, and by the sound principles upon which they run an international, multibillion-dollar corporation that is much larger and more complex than the Amway that Jay and I ran.

By the time Jay's four children and my four children started approaching high school age, we both thought that at least some of them would one day want to work in the family business. So we thought each of them should at least start by working in various departments to get to know Amway and how it runs. Each of our children participated in what was planned to be a five-year experience of working in every Amway department for about six months. They worked in our warehouses, manufacturing plants, research and development laboratories, and offices—both day and night shifts. Some of them started this training in summer jobs during high school, sweeping floors and mowing lawns. My oldest son spent some time as a tour guide. Using his middle name, he introduced himself to guests as Dick Marvin, so he wouldn't be recognized as my son. He, along with the rest, pushed a broom and learned what it was like to work on an assembly line. Of course, the jobs during each child's five-year experience became more complex.

In the early 1990s I started having even more serious heart problems, which required bypass surgery. My illnesses prevented me from being able to work. By that time Dick had been working at Amway for about fifteen years, having been vice president of international for the last five. He had become restless and left the company for a couple of years to start a business of his own; nevertheless, I asked him to return and fill my position. Jay later developed health challenges and became ready to pass on his daily responsibilities, so a few years after Dick succeeded me, Jay and I decided that his son Steve was the most qualified to assume the duties of chairman.

———

WHEN DICK AND STEVE took over for Jay and me, they stepped right up and handled some difficult challenges. For example, they had to steer the company through a sales decline in the late 1990s. With sales falling, Dick and Steve also had to make the very tough decision to reduce the workforce and make a number of other management and structural changes. I remember at the time Dick telling me that we needed to borrow money for terminations, because we weren't making enough to cover them.

I said, "Dick, I thought we were going to reduce our costs by laying off people."

He said, "Not if we're going to do it right. We need to have proper separations, pay people for their service, and help them get new jobs."

Looking back, I realize Jay and I had been unwilling to make the decision to downsize. We just didn't want to deal with it. We figured things were going to turn around next month or next year and we'd be okay. Dick and Steve not only made the tough decisions, but they also handled things the right way and soon turned Amway back into a profitable company.

When Dick took over as president, he said, "I'll give myself about six years in this job, and then I'll be ready for a change." And that proved to be true—although he stayed for ten years before he was ready to leave. By then our youngest son, Doug, having done the training, lived in Brussels and then the United Kingdom as general manager of that area, and worked his way up to senior vice president of Asia Pacific and Global Distributor Relations and then chief operating officer of Amway, was ready to take over.

Dick was ready for a new challenge, and was eager to grow the company he had started before returning to Amway. He did that, and now has several other companies that he and his wife, Betsy, own and operate. He is also the chairman of RDV Corporation, our family's office, which handles all of our numerous DeVos family business activities outside Amway and the Magic. He has also filled a whole new role by taking the family leadership position, and has added structure to our family's interest in encouraging generational succession so we will continue to be a flourishing family.

But beyond managing our business interests outside of Amway and the Magic, a really important function of our family office is to bring our family members together on a regular basis to meet and decide on important family matters. We formed the DeVos Family Council, which is made up of our children and their spouses and meets four times a year. The Family Council just approved a family constitution that essentially captures our family mission and values. We see this as a way to encourage the important principles Helen and I have lived by and make sure they get carried on throughout the generations. The Family Council also articulates how the family will work together in managing our shared financial interests and our philanthropy.

We also have the Family Assembly, which involves all three generations—Helen and I, our children and their spouses, and some of our grandchildren—and meets once a year, with all family members expected to attend. When grandchildren turn sixteen, they are inducted into the Family Assembly in a formal ceremony that everyone attends. An aunt or uncle makes a presentation of their achievements, reminds them of their responsibility as they go forward, and affirms them as a member of the Family Assembly. They are then eligible to be invited to attend the meeting, where important family matters are discussed. They are able to vote in the meetings at age twenty-five, after they have met additional qualifications for taking on this added responsibility.

Through our family office, we've also developed a program for the grandchildren that teaches business principles, and skills such as leadership and teamwork, and passes on values that our family has found to be keys to success in life and in business. These are the values that Helen and I grew up with and have lived by, and we believe it's important for our children to encourage their children to carry on these same values.

I also think there is interest among some of the grandchildren in working at Amway. If they're serious about it, they need to earn a four-year college degree and work for a number of years at another company before they are eligible to come back and apply for a job at Amway.

Perhaps one reason a family business has been so important to me is that family itself has always been important to me—from the family I grew up in, to my marriage to Helen, to the children we raised to be successful adults, and finally to the grandchildren I love to watch grow up. I've already shared with you my childhood memories of my loving and nurturing family, which helped shape my life. I must have learned a lot from that rewarding experience, because I was blessed to become a husband and father in the same kind of family in which I grew up.

And just as I started a lifelong partnership with Jay Van Andel after he gave me a ride to school, a short ride in a car also was how I first met Helen. I was riding in a friend's car through a neighborhood in southeast Grand Rapids on a pleasant fall day in 1946 when we spotted two young ladies walking together. My friend knew them because they were going to the same college we were, so we stopped and offered them a ride. They said they were nearly home and could just keep walking, but after a little more urging they climbed in.

It was a short ride—about a block—until we'd reached the house where they were headed. We dropped them off and one girl gave a polite thank-you and left, but I stopped the second one to ask who the first girl was. She grabbed one of my textbooks and wrote "Helen Van Wesep," adding Helen's phone number as well. We still have that book, but I must confess that I gave her phone number to a friend and he called her.

However, we got to know each other and, after some time had passed, I finally gave her a call. It was a few years after our flying school days, but I still had connections, so our first date was an airplane ride over and around Grand Rapids on a beautiful, clear Sunday afternoon. We continued dating after that, but were dating others as well. After a spell of dating we wouldn't see each other for a while, and then I'd call her again. It kind of kept going like that until one day in late summer, when Helen was visiting a teacher friend in a cottage close to where Jay and I had docked our power boat, and she took her friend's two little girls for a walk and they decided they wanted to look at the boats.

I was there to take my uncle and aunt for a boat ride when I saw them coming down the dock, and once again I found myself asking her if she'd like a ride! The little girls were excited, so the three of them climbed aboard and once again we went for a short ride—to the gas dock so I could fill up, and back because I'd already finished my ride with my relatives. That encounter made me want to see Helen again, and this time I realized I had fallen in love with her. By the end of that year we were talking marriage.

That was before the days of marriage counseling by a pastor or other professional, but Helen and I already knew we were compatible in the ways that mattered most: besides loving each other, we shared a common faith in Jesus Christ and had grown up with similar family backgrounds and values. It was on that solid foundation and with appreciation of one another's abilities, characters, and outlook on life that we built a marriage that has lasted more than sixty years and is still going strong! We had four children, whom we love dearly and of whom we're very proud, and they in turn married and blessed us with sixteen grand-children, and now we have two darling great-granddaughters as well. When I've been asked over the years why our children have all turned out so well I can only say God has blessed our efforts as parents. I also give a lot of the credit to Helen, who was the stay-at-home mom when I had to devote so much of my time to building a business that required evening work and travel. I'm just extremely grateful they're all such capable, hardworking, and generous adults.

One of the first things I did when our children were growing up was to block out family time when I set up my calendar for the year. First, birthdays were plugged in, and any particular school activities they'd be engaged in, as well as sports activities as they got older. Holidays always were specially entered, and many of those were celebrated with our extended family. Family was important to us, and we made every effort to focus on being and doing things together. That effort, I decided early on, negated my choosing golf as a sport. Golf is not a family sport when your family is young. Fathers of young children in my day usually played golf alone or with a bunch of guys on Saturdays. I just felt that playing golf meant walking away from your family every Saturday morning, and I couldn't do that.

However, in spite of my early misadventure with Jay in our sailboat, I continued to have a love affair with sailing. Sometime in the mid-1960s, Helen and I had taken a weekend away and stayed at a little "boatel" on the river in Saugatuck, Michigan. The second evening we were there we were sitting on our balcony when a sailboat came in wanting dockage, and I hurried off to offer my help with the lines. As we were tying up, I learned that the boat was owned by three men and it was for sale. (*Three* owners? No wonder it was for sale!) I took the opportunity to check it out below and on deck, and talked with the sailors about how the boat sailed, etc. The conversation took a whole new turn when I came back and told Helen it was for sale. She knew I had loved sailing and had talked about having a sailboat again someday, but it seemed as if an opportunity had thrust itself upon us unawares! It had been just the two of us for a couple's "time away," and suddenly we seemed to be faced with a decision that could change our lives . . . in an interesting way! We made a date with the owners for a trial run, and looked forward to the day.

When *the* day came, we took the two boys with us, but almost threw in the towel when we saw the lake. The waves were really big—ten-footers, the sailors on the boat told us happily. I wasn't quite so happy because I knew Helen was apprehensive, and the boys were pretty wide-eyed as well. But we climbed aboard, put on life jackets (they were pretty old, and had big collars that made them clumsy to wear), and started out the channel. So far so good—but then we hit the lake and the boat heeled. I saw Helen sitting on the high side with one arm clutching the winch to hold on, and the other on one of the boys, whom she had ordered to sit on the deck, with firm instructions that they should hold on to one another.

And where were the sailor-salesmen? Up on the boom, leaning into the billowing mainsail, having a great old time. When we finally came about and headed back to the dock, the guys and I were wondering what Helen's reaction would be—after all, if we bought the boat she'd be co-owner, and she hadn't looked particularly happy during the run. But she surprised us all (she says she bowed to the inevitable) and thought the boat would be a great thing for our family, and from that day on we became boaters.

That decision had unintended consequences, all good, that extend to this day. Although we had kind of backed into it, sailing turned out to be a great sport for our family because it was an endeavor we could all share in and enjoy together. And it naturally teaches responsibility. Because living space is limited, clothing had to be picked up and stowed so no one would stumble on it; bunks needed to be made up right away so we'd have a place to sit. Our children learned quickly that cleaning was part of what you do when you have a boat, and that meant outside as well. Each morning the deck needed mopping, rails needed wiping, and the boat needed to be tidied up to get it ready for the day. And the dog had to be taken out—yes, we even added her to our boating family.

Our boat gave us opportunities to go places and do things in a unique way. Many summers we'd spend three weeks traveling on Lake Michigan, going from port to port up the west coast. We usually made only fifty miles or so a day motoring. (Another thing the family learned about sailing was that there's no such thing as going straight from point A to point B, so we motored a lot. Having a sail was an *event*!) I'd try to start early because the kids would get restless, and by 2 p.m. they wanted to get off the boat and play.

But if the lake was flat and we were just cruising along, I'd use that time to show them how to sand a rail to prepare it to accept varnish, and how to apply the varnish. It was a wooden boat, and there were plenty of rails to work on, but the kids were always ready and willing to help. When we reached our destination we would tie up in that small harbor town and go ashore to play ball or just walk around the town and shop or buy ice-cream cones or some fudge. They all remember that fondly, as well as the towns—Pentwater, White Lake, Ludington, Leland, Frankfort, Charlevoix, Petoskey, Harbor Springs, and points north.

But traveling from port to port also taught our children about planning and the importance of getting an early start.

Running in fog or difficult conditions that might come up later in the day taught them how important it can be to start early and get to your destination on time, so that if the weather does get bad you don't have to fight it—you're already in your slip and tied up for the night. And it's just the family on the move— no distractions then with TV or cell phones or computers, just a time to be together and have some conversation about where we are, what's happening during the day, plans for tomorrow, navigation strategies, checking for the next lighthouse or mark—just talking, together. Kids never get very far away on a boat, so you talk together about a variety of subjects that are just part of life. I hope these conversations and the experiences we provided our children had some impact—and somewhere along the line, they even learned to sail.

———

IS LEADERSHIP TEACHABLE? OUR children watched leaders, but becoming a leader didn't happen as part of their school curriculum. They picked it up as they went along. As I reflect, I think that leadership is discovered by doing. People who are in business often discover that they have leadership ability they never thought they had. Happily, my children all ended up being good leaders. I think that's sort of by osmosis as they watched and heard known leaders speak about how they handled different situations. Exposure to leaders showing leadership has an impact. My son Dan did a thirteen-year stint at Amway, focusing on the distributor relations area, spending the last thirteen months living in Tokyo with his family, working the (at that time) eight Pacific markets. Upon returning to the United States, he decided to take the bold step of going off on his own to become an entrepreneur and has since that time established a couple of dozen automobile and Fox Powersports dealerships up and down West Michigan. He is the owner of a minor league hockey team, has other business interests as well, and we recently tapped his business talents to oversee the Orlando Magic for the family.

My daughter, Cheri, learned the Amway business too, was vice president of our growing worldwide cosmetics business, and spent several years helping us oversee the Magic—the latter while raising five children. She has also served on the Alticor/ Amway board of directors and as a trustee of Hope College, her alma mater. She is definitely a leader in her own right. Our daughters-in-law caught the leadership bug as well: Betsy with her political leadership locally and nationally, and her effort to expand educational choice across America; Pamella starting her own successful business in the fashion industry; and Maria passionately leading numerous community initiatives to benefit West Michigan.

We didn't have any question about our children's abilities to be effective leaders or to function well in life. They knew how to respect others. Helen and I impressed on our children that all people are worthwhile, important, because we're all created by God. If you don't respect others, how can they respect you? A good leader earns respect by giving respect, but must also be an honest, trustworthy person whose word is his bond. Others are always treated kindly by someone who respects them; they are never to be disparaged because they didn't go to the right school, or didn't have the same opportunities as you. That doesn't make them any less worthy or important or able. Our children learned in the Amway business that all people have ability. Growing up in an Amway family is a tremendously positive experience.

Helen and I were fortunate to be in agreement about raising children. That's the nice part of marrying somebody who has the same roots of family and faith. The challenge comes when parents have very different backgrounds and need to find common ground before they can pass on anything meaningful to their children. But if you marry someone as I did, who comes from the same background, you already know where you're in agreement, even before you are married. But one thing Helen and I did *not* have in common was that she was an only child, so sometimes I had to help her out when she showed concern about our bustling household of four children.

She would say to me, "Is this how it's supposed to be in a family? Is this how I should expect them to act?"

I'd say, "It's normal, honey, don't worry; yes, they're *supposed* to hit each other now and then."

When I wrote *Believe!* all those years ago, I included a chapter about my belief in family. As I wrote then, and still believe, "the vitality of our American system . . . depends on what occurs in the living rooms, dining rooms, dens and backyards of millions of ordinary, modest American homes." I look back on my own childhood family and know this is true when I think about our

Both of my
grandfathers were
small business
owners and had
delivery routes
for the sale of
their products.

A photo of me at age two,
the start of an amazing journey.

A portrait of my
sister Bernice
and me with our
loving parents.

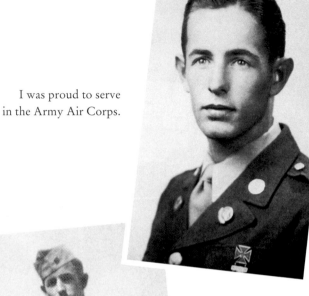

I was proud to serve in the Army Air Corps.

Jay and I served miles apart in World War II but returned home with an even deeper friendship and commitment to doing something significant in an energized, victorious America.

Jay and I didn't know how to fly at the time, but that didn't prevent us from starting Wolverine Air Service.

When Jay and I started Wolverine Air Service, our local airport hadn't officially opened so we equipped our plane, similar to this one, with pontoons and used the nearby Grand River as the "landing strip" for our students.

Jay and I were proud of the matching flight jackets we wore in our humble office at Wolverine Air Service.

Despite our sailor caps, Jay and I knew little about sailing when this photo was taken of us aboard our thirty-eight-foot sailboat, *Elizabeth,* in port on our way to Cuba.

NUTRILITE SENIOR KEY CONFERENCE

YOSEMITE NATIONAL PARK

May   1956

Jay and Betty (left) and Helen and I (right) are pictured here during a Nutrilite Conference with Walter and Evelyn Bass, who later became two of our first Amway distributors.

Just months after the founding of Amway I was busy giving speeches.

My father presented the keys to the driver of the van we thought would be the beginning of delivery routes for our products. We soon learned that Amway was much more than a product delivery company.

Amway received a lot of national media attention through the years, but publicity in the early days started on local TV like this show.

Jay and I held one of our first big Amway distributor conventions in the Black and Silver Room at what was then the Civic Auditorium in downtown Grand Rapids, Michigan.

After a few years, I started to become identified with the familiar red, white, and blue Amway logo.

Jay and I had our portrait taken in the first office
building constructed on the growing Amway
complex in Ada, Michigan.

In the early years of Amway Jay and I often shared the stage at
distributor meetings.

The album cover of the recording of my award-winning speech, "Selling America."

Jay and I believed in the American Way and, of course, felt it appropriate to raise the flag at our new World Headquarters building, which we initially called the Center of Free Enterprise.

Jay and I started Amway Manufacturing with our first production of L.O.C., and I never lost interest in going into our plants to talk with employees and see our latest products.

Developing new products for home care was important to the growth of Amway in the early years.

Jay and I were excited to cut the ribbon on another addition to the Amway complex.

Jay and I were proud to pose in front of our new Center of Free Enterprise building, which now serves as Amway World Headquarters, in Ada, Michigan.

We were honored that then U.S. congressman Gerald Ford helped us cut the ribbon at the dedication of the Amway Grand Plaza Hotel in Grand Rapids, Michigan.

I am a regular attendee at the Orlando Magic games. Here I am chatting before a game with Nick Anderson, who was the very first draft pick of the Orlando Magic when the franchise was founded in 1989.

By the early 1980s, attendance at Amway conventions had become impressive as a growing number of people wanted to seize the opportunity to be independent business owners.

I was a great supporter and admirer of President Reagan and was thrilled to be able to share a stage with him and Mrs. Reagan.

Both I and my family were honored and excited to meet President and Mrs. Reagan.

My speech became the traditional finale to our annual Amway conventions in Grand Rapids, Michigan.

I spoke to thousands of groups all over the world during my lifetime, including this 40,000-strong crowd of Amway distributors gathered at the Tokyo Dome in 2004.

I've been photographed many times behind a podium, but those familiar with my speaking style know I prefer to get out from behind it and walk around the stage.

More comfortable on the water than in it, Helen adapted to a life of boating ever since we purchased our first *Windquest*. Many of our fondest family memories have occurred aboard a boat.

cozy home, our conversations and devotions around the dinner table, my father's encouraging words, the discussions with my mother while doing dishes after dinner, or even playing Ping-Pong with my little sister Jan. I know this is true when I am filled with thankfulness at how my children share the values and faith that Helen and I had tried to instill. And I see that the future of our family is strong as I watch each of my grandchildren grow and begin to develop their own leadership talents and make their mark in the world.

CHAPTER THIRTEEN

A Sinner Saved by Grace

T HE AMWAY HELICOPTER APPEARED to barely clear the two towers of the Mackinac Bridge, which connects Michigan's Lower and Upper Peninsulas. We hovered toward a landing on the little grass airstrip on Mackinac Island. I was arriving to fulfill an invitation to speak at the Detroit Chamber of Commerce annual meeting and was prepared with some facts about our Amway business for this crowd of successful businesspeople. But mostly I was planning to talk to them about being life enrichers.

A few hundred people were gathered in the elegant old ballroom of the Grand Hotel, with its views of lushly landscaped grounds and Lake Huron beyond. They were enjoying their lunch as they awaited my speech. The person introducing me went on and on about my "many accomplishments as one of the state's leading entrepreneurs"—he was simply referring to items in my biography, so I couldn't really blame him, but his introduction was the most lengthy and flowery I had ever received. I felt like standing up and saying, "Are you going to make this speech today or am I?"

Standing at the podium and looking out over the crowd after my grand introduction, I thanked the man for his generous words, but added, "That introduction really doesn't describe me. Let me tell you who I really am. I'm a sinner, saved by grace—a Christian, saved by Jesus Christ. That's who I really am." This all happened more than twenty years ago, and I've often introduced myself that way since, even with non-Christian groups of people. Not to try to convert them, but simply to state who I am.

I once introduced myself that way to a very devout Jewish group, and after I finished a woman came up to me and asked, "Would you come and speak to my group at our synagogue?" She didn't seem to take offense at my public proclamation of my Christian faith. It's not my business to offend people, but to encourage them. Also it's not within my power to convert anyone. Only the Lord can do that.

I was born into a Christian family, so I was brought up in a home of faith. All my grandparents, who came to America from the Netherlands, were Christians as well. Although Grandpa

DeVos had no faith when he came to America, he did become a strong Christian as an adult. (Grandpa's mother died when he was a boy, and his father disappeared, so at the age of eleven he somehow came up with enough money to buy a boat ticket and left the Netherlands hoping for a better life in America, the land of opportunity.) Grandpa wasn't a Christian when he married and had his family, but one day the pastor of Eastern Avenue Christian Reformed Church in Grand Rapids knocked on his door and shared Christ with him, and Grandpa gave his life to the Lord and became a Christian—and eventually the rest of his family joined him.

I grew up in a neighborhood of Dutch immigrants, who were Protestants. On the west side of the Grand River, which divides our city, was a settlement of Polish immigrants, who were Catholics. That was pretty much the extent of religious diversity in Grand Rapids when I was growing up. We played pickup football and baseball games against our Polish neighbors and even got into some fights with them when our rivalry became a little too heated. But faith was a part of all of our lives. The Polish people went to their Catholic churches, and the Dutch people went to a Reformed or Christian Reformed church. Oftentimes there was a Reformed church on one corner and a Christian Reformed church on the other—the Christian Reformed Church (CRC) had split from the Reformed Church in America (RCA). Today I'm involved with others in an effort to reunite these two Christian denominations.

Helen grew up in the CRC, and we still are members of

LaGrave Avenue CRC in Grand Rapids. But when I was growing up my family was Protestant Reformed, an offshoot of the CRC. The original church was a substantial brick building that had a large sanctuary with spacious balconies on either side and seated, as I can best recall, about eight hundred members. It dominated the corner of Franklin and Fuller Streets in Grand Rapids. The church was started by Herman Hoeksema, a CRC pastor who had some disagreement with his fellow brethren over interpretations of certain passages of scripture. He was adamant in his views and left the CRC, taking a number of members with him to begin yet another denomination. Grandma Dekker decided she agreed with Rev. Hoeksema so she became a member of the Protestant Reformed Church (PRC), and took the children—including my mother—with her. Grandpa, my mother's father, stayed with the CRC and attended church alone every Sunday.

Theological differences don't just divide congregations—they can even divide families. Marriages can come close to breaking up over church differences. Relatives can be at odds with each other over a point of theology. Three generations of us belonged to the PRC, but eventually my parents, my sisters, and I returned to the CRC. My mother said later that she couldn't imagine how they could have let her father walk off to church alone all those years, but Grandpa knew with whom he wanted to stand, and he refused to jump ship.

Most kids from my neighborhood can remember attending catechism classes, typically held on Wednesday evenings, where young people were taught in depth the creeds to which we subscribed. We also affirmed the Apostle's Creed, which stated in brief the abiding beliefs of Christians everywhere—in God our Father, Jesus Christ our Savior, and the Holy Spirit, our guide to all truth.

I went with my family to church every Sunday—morning and evening. Sunday was a day set aside for worship. God had commanded us to keep Sunday holy, and many families were restrictive about what activities they would allow on the rest of the day. For example, we could throw a ball around in the front yard, but we didn't go to ball games that were played on Sunday. Our family considered Sunday a day for family interaction: our Sunday-evening tradition was to go to one of the uncle and aunt's homes for supper, and then to attend the evening service together. When I was in Christian High, classmates would often come over after the evening service—Mother would have refreshments for us, and we would play games, listen to the radio, or just hang out together and talk. Few businesses in town were open on Sunday to lure us out, but we never felt we were being restricted or kept from going out if we wanted to. Because our house was always open to my friends, Jay came over often and got to know my mother well. She was wonderful and took us all under her wing.

In addition to the influence of church and family, the Christian schools I attended helped me construct a world and life view that became my foundation in life. Geography was the study of the world that God created. When discussing relationships, we considered that all people are created by God, so we should always respect each other. If a student excelled in sports or played a musical instrument well or was outstanding in the classroom, it was acknowledged that their talent was a special gift from God. It was because my parents believed strongly in a Christian education that they put aside money, even in those hard times, so I could attend Christian schools; and it was at Grand Rapids Christian High that I met Jay Van Andel. Can you imagine how different my life would have been if I hadn't been in that school?

I believe that providence put us there, and Jay and I became best friends.

In Reformed churches we were given the sacrament of baptism as infants, as a sign that we are included in God's covenant and people. Around the age of graduation from high school it was customary to make a public profession of our faith before our church congregation. Since I didn't always agree with what I was hearing from our church pulpit, I decided to delay making a public profession of faith. I knew I was totally committed to Christ but I was conflicted about some of the theology embraced by my church, so I waited.

After returning from military service, I spoke with another pastor and shared my dilemma with him. After hearing me out, he said, "You know what? Your God is too small! Just because you don't understand how He can know beforehand what you're going to do and still give you total free will, doesn't mean He can't do it. He's the Supreme Being of the universe, and our minds are only human." I thought that through, and realized my pastor friend was right. The God I had worshipped growing up was all-powerful, all-knowing, and ever-present, but I had unwittingly been seeing Him in human dimensions.

When I returned to the God I already knew, I was ready to declare my Christian faith first to my church congregation and then to the world.

I continue to make my decisions based on religious principles. The way we choose to live our lives starts with the conviction that God is real and values all people equally. We honor this equality in Amway by respecting all people and not restricting anyone from being a distributor.

It's what people do that counts, and proves what they are. Whatever their color, education, or ethnicity, they all have an equal opportunity to join our business. We founded Amway on that principle—a distributor moves ahead only when he or she runs an honest business and helps somebody else move ahead. No one may gain at the expense of another.

Many leading Amway distributors have been very public about their Christian faith. I finally cautioned them: "I don't want to come to an Amway meeting and hear a sermon any more than I want to go to church and hear about Amway. So let's make sure we keep both of these things distinctly separate. Who knows what'll happen in someone's life because of their association with you and others in Amway? But let's not force the issue. If you want to talk to your people about your faith, do it privately—not at an Amway function."

After that, when distributors held their meetings on weekends, many offered separate church services on Sunday, open to anyone wishing to attend. It was not part of the business meetings. That arrangement has served us well. Many different pastors have spoken at those Sunday services and have helped people find a Christian faith to believe and live by. However, in my speeches to audiences outside Amway, I still introduce myself as a Christian and let people know how my faith leads my life.

———

AS STRONGLY AS I believe in free enterprise, optimism, and other principles I've shared in this book, I believe in one thing even more strongly: a personal God, in His Son, Jesus Christ, and in the mission of His church. I've never tried to force my personal faith on others but I am willing to declare my faith publicly. If my faith has been such a rewarding and fulfilling part of my life, how could I not share such good news with others? Because I've been so open about my Christian convictions, some have asked me if Amway is a Christian organization. Amway has a lot of wonderful Christian people in it, but a company cannot be Christian, only people can be Christian. As an international company, Amway today operates in countries in which the majority of citizens are members of religions other than Christianity, and all are welcome to enjoy the AMWAY opportunity.

So while I've never used the gospel to promote my business, I cannot turn off my beliefs when I leave church on Sunday. I am a Christian by faith and experience and cannot make decisions or take positions that are not compatible with my faith. My role as a successful businessperson who has achieved material wealth has never led me to believe that I no longer had a need for God's grace and guidance. All I have materially comes from God, and only in worship of God can money bring real happiness.

Looking back at my life and how God has so richly blessed me, I can only ask, "Why me, Lord?" I can only acknowledge that all I have is truly God's and for some reason He has made me His steward over it. I believe in maintaining a sense of dependence on God. That is what true faith and humility are all about.

I just thank God that I grew up in a home and community that introduced me to my Christian faith and encouraged me to practice my faith daily. The practice has never been a burden but instead has resulted in a feeling of great joy, comfort, and peace that I would hope everyone could experience.

CHAPTER FOURTEEN

Our Town Built on Life Enrichers

IMAGINE BEING ASKED, OUT of the blue, to join a committee tasked with raising millions of dollars. That was once my invitation from our mayor, the goal being to raise money to restore our city to its past glory. Like most cities during the 1970s, Grand Rapids was losing money and population to the suburbs and was in dire need of revitalization. One of our main streets, Monroe Avenue, had a couple of aging department stores and dime stores, but a lot of empty storefronts. The once-bustling Pantlind Hotel had become seedy. A few buses still hummed through the city, but nothing exciting was happening downtown. The hub of activity had moved to suburban neighborhoods and shopping malls.

As I've already pointed out, a community benefits from a sense of ownership by its citizens. If we are proud of our city and want to see it prosper, we can make a positive change where we live. I've also talked about the benefits of being life enrichers, and how that kind of positive attitude and action helps everyone succeed. But those attitudes were rare forty years ago when our town was being abandoned and seriously needed help.

One man stepped forward to get the ball rolling—Lyman Parks, the first black mayor of Grand Rapids. He formed a committee of business and community leaders to raise funds to improve the existing convention center and to build a music hall. An improved center was important to bring more convention business to the city, and a music hall was needed to house and showcase the growing arts groups in town, particularly the already well-established Grand Rapids Symphony Orchestra, which had been performing in our original aging civic center.

I was asked to serve on the committee and was given the additional assignment to serve with a prominent local bank president, Dick Gillette, on the fund-raising committee. We hired a Chicago architect who specialized in symphony halls to design our music hall—the first ever for Grand Rapids—and Dick and I went to all the "old money" in Grand Rapids to try to raise the $6 million to build it—a substantial amount in those days. We received next to nothing.

We then held a by-invitation-only dinner party at Amway for

potential donors to hear our presentation for the hall, which focused on its potential to be a meeting place downtown on the Grand River. We explained how, thanks to the American Indians who had lived there before us, all trails led to the Grand River. When roads were built, they followed the trails so they, too, could bring people in from all directions to a meeting place on the river. The theme of our fund-raising campaign became "A Meeting Place on the Grand." Raising $6 million was a tough pull—people weren't in the habit of giving as they are today. I had approached several wealthy families, offering them the idea that, for a contribution of a million dollars, the music hall could be named for them. I had no takers. People in those days simply did not think in terms of giving large donations or putting names on buildings in recognition of a citizen's generosity.

Dick Gillette finally said to me, "I really don't want any of those people's names on that building. I want *your* name on that building. You represent the next generation of givers. You're the new guy on the block, an up-and-comer, and I want you to be a million-dollar giver. Then we can put *your* name on the building."

Although as a businessman my interest focused more on the convention center, Helen was interested in the arts and was then serving on the board of the Grand Rapids Symphony. While giving a substantial amount toward the building of a music hall was one thing, agreeing to have it named for us was quite another. We hesitated a long while, discussing it seriously between ourselves and then with a few of our close friends. We finally decided to say yes to the naming, sincerely hoping not to be perceived as showing off or being on an ego trip. So eventually the city's new music hall bore the DeVos name, and it still does.

That contribution was significant to us as our first million-dollar gift. But more significant for the city was Dick Gillette's vision of going to the next generation. "From this time on," he said, "we can go to different people in this community, and with your example, begin to ask for big money. It will set the pace for a whole new community of givers." He very clearly saw that this could be the first of many such projects and the beginning of naming new buildings for citizen donors.

And Dick was right—this project *was* the beginning of a giving period in Grand Rapids that we hadn't seen before.

One idea sparked another. Our new convention center needed nearby hotels. At that time, we had no ballroom in our city for celebrations or major events, but ideas were forming for a possible new hotel with meeting rooms, ballrooms, restaurants, etc. If we were serious about restoring our downtown, we needed to address our lack of such facilities. I was asked to contact the Hiltons and others in the hotel business about considering putting a hotel in downtown Grand Rapids, but they all said they were building near airports now, not downtowns.

That's when I said, "Jay, why don't *we* do it? We could, you know!" He agreed, so we went to work. We didn't build a new hotel; instead, Amway bought the old downtown Pantlind and proceeded to transform the aging building into the luxurious hotel known since as the Amway Grand Plaza. We hired a team of Grand Rapids architects, Marvin DeWinter and Gretchen Minhaar, along with the Dan Vos Construction Company from Ada, Michigan, to build the project. The original hotel rooms were too small by modern standards, so every two rooms were combined to create one. In the basement, the old sewer, water, and steam lines were replaced. We hired Carleton Varney, a high-profile designer from New York, to redo the interior since everything had to be refinished or replaced to transform a dilapidated relic into a modern four-star hotel. He did it up in great style—with gold leaf on the lobby ceiling, plush carpets, rich fabrics, and fine furniture throughout. Our friend Ambassador Peter Secchia leased space for two restaurants—one for fine dining, which became the often-honored 1913 Room, and the other, Tootsie's, which was more laid-back.

Redoing the hotel was a satisfying adventure, but we had never thought of ourselves as hoteliers. We had mostly thought to restore the hotel to improve Grand Rapids by showing faith in the future of downtown. The community immediately saw the potential of the Amway Grand Plaza Hotel to be the hub of the city, and meetings, weddings, and other major celebrations were booked. At its dedication, President Ford said, "The city is being reborn."

Our new hotel opened in 1981, and within months Jay and I were considering constructing an adjoining twenty-nine-story tower. The tower was already designed, but we thought perhaps we should pause and take a breath before deciding to go ahead with a major new building. We had nothing solid to go on regarding demand for it—the demand was all geared around the eventuality of the potential new convention center being planned by the city. After deliberating awhile, we decided one day we were never going to have enough information to say we're positively going to have the business to support a new tower, so I said once again, "Jay, why don't we just go ahead and do it? We could, you know!"

He agreed, so we did.

Two years later the Amway Grand Plaza Hotel boasted a new tower—contemporary in design and amenities, with rooms designed to please customers who preferred that style of décor.

We also realized that we needed people to begin living downtown for it to remain viable, so our next project was the first condominium building in Grand Rapids, which we named Plaza Towers. The people who filled it just loved being downtown. Unfortunately, unknown to us, the out-of-state builder had cut corners and the owners began to have serious water problems, both interior and exterior. Other issues surfaced as well, so after serious discussion, one of the solutions suggested was simply to tear the building down. The cost of tearing the building down would have actually been less than the cost of remodeling, but Jay said firmly, "We're not tearer-downers. We're builders. Let's go build it up again." After that there was nothing more to be said. Once again, we restored a building to make it beautiful and livable, and the residents were most gracious about moving elsewhere until the place was done.

The revolution in downtown Grand Rapids continued—one fund-raiser at a time, one building following on the heels of the one just completed. Anyone who grew up in Grand Rapids and left thirty years ago would not recognize the skyline if they saw it today. Since our hotel was completed in 1981, the new downtown buildings include an arena, public museum, a downtown campus of Grand Valley State University, a new convention center to replace the one already outgrown, a JW Marriott hotel, and what today is known as the Medical Mile: the Van Andel Institute, Meijer Heart Center, the Lemmen-Holton Cancer Pavilion, the Helen DeVos Children's Hospital, the Cook-DeVos medical building of GVSU, and the Secchia Center, part of the School of Human Medicine of Michigan State University.

The twelve-thousand-seat Van Andel Arena has attracted thousands of people to downtown. It has become the home of the Grand Rapids Griffins hockey team, and has hosted concerts by some of the biggest names in entertainment. A civic committee had gained the city's approval for an arena downtown and then acted to raise the funds through a private-public partnership, and what had been a dream for many years became a reality. With the completion of a major hotel and an arena, Grand Rapids could also accommodate a larger convention center, which I was honored to help fund. Now DeVos Place graces the shores of the Grand River as well.

The rebirth of Grand Rapids today is probably most noted for the hospitals and medical buildings that have sprouted along Michigan Street during the past two decades. When Jay was considering leaving as his legacy a medical research center, I spoke with him about the importance of the center being located in the downtown area. We had become seen as the pioneers in developing our city, so I thought it only fitting that Jay establish this research center—Van Andel Institute—in the heart of Grand Rapids and near our large downtown hospital, Spectrum Health. He agreed, and was able to secure a site just west of the hospital. It was there he built a beautiful building for research.

Soon after came the twelve-story Meijer Heart Center. That fund-raising campaign—chaired by Spectrum board member Bob Hooker, community leader Earl Holton, and our son Dick—was the largest in our city's history at that time, with the late Fred Meijer and his wife, Lena, providing the lead gift. This heart center has become widely known for its excellent facilities, skillful staff, and outstanding quality of care. The first heart transplant in Grand Rapids was performed in 2011 in the Meijer Heart Center. We've been able to attract world-leading heart specialists to the center, so the future looks bright for our city to continue to be a destination for world-class heart care.

Next to the Meijer Heart Center is the Helen DeVos Children's Hospital, which first opened its doors on January 11, 2011. Dr. Luis Tomatis, of whom you'll hear more later, had been very involved in trying to get a children's hospital in Grand Rapids, and had been successful in getting Spectrum Health to add a wing for women and children, which opened in 1993. Although the two seemed to be a logical blend, after several years of coexisting it became apparent that each area had its own needs and would be better off in separate facilities. Because of the ever-increasing child-patient population, the added wing was no longer large enough to accommodate all the children who were coming for treatment. Once again Dr. Tomatis was looking for an adequate building for specialized treatment for children—one that was meant for child-sized patients from the ground up, and would be totally child-friendly. Since the DeVos name had been on the original children's hospital, he thought we might be interested in helping again. We were, but this time I said I wanted it named the *Helen* DeVos Children's Hospital. Our children agreed and together gave the lead gift. Dr. Tomatis got the ball rolling, and now there's a big, blue building atop Michigan Street Hill where children continue to receive expert, individualized care from specialists.

But, looking back, I think one of my proudest accomplishments in the medical area is not a building. It was in becoming a member of the board of Butterworth Hospital in downtown Grand Rapids that a whole new era in my life began. Butterworth was one of two large hospitals in our city, the other being Blodgett, and there was a good bit of rivalry between the two, which led to duplication of services and purchasing inefficiencies. When the backers of Blodgett began to talk about putting up a new building, I said to Bill Gonzalez, then president of Butterworth, "What do you think about trying to merge these two hospitals?"

"Well," he said, "you're not the first to come up with that idea."

I said, "I know, but why don't we try it again anyway?" He said he'd work with me if I really wanted to try, so I replied,

"Let's go. If we can pull this off, it may be the most significant thing we ever do." First, I convinced the members of the Butterworth board to get behind me; then the chairman of the board at Blodgett bought into the idea and brought his members along, and the process began. We weren't too far into it before the Federal Trade Commission challenged the merger, saying it had the potential to be a monopoly on medical care and costs in Grand Rapids. Because FTC approval was required to merge two hospitals in the same community, I had to testify at a trial in Lansing, our state capital.

The FTC representative said to me, "You're a competitive, free enterprise guy. Why don't you want these two hospitals to compete with each other? Competition would keep costs down." I said, "You know, you're right . . . *if* these were two competing hospitals that were owned by *different* entities, but these are not. They're both owned by the public—the same people, the same community of Grand Rapids. If they were merged there'd be no monopoly because the ownership is the same." We won the case, and a merged hospital system named Spectrum was born.

The judge who decided the case wrote a chapter in his book many years later about what had happened since the merger. He wrote at length about "the growth of the medical complex and quality of care—how our prices didn't go up any more than that of any other hospital, but the quality of care did." Our level of service went up because of the doctors we were able to attract, and more people in the region began to come to us for medical care.

I'm grateful that the renewal of downtown Grand Rapids took off, and that the whole community supported it. It doesn't matter how good an idea is if you can't get support for it from others. I've learned that oftentimes all it takes to get people moving toward a goal is for someone to show interest and offer help. We're grateful that we've been helpful in creating a culture of giving in our community.

Today, when people moving into Grand Rapids ask me, "How do I meet people?" I say, "Just go to the nearest fundraiser and buy a seat. Let people know you're a giver, and you'll suddenly have a tableful of new friends." I'm kidding, of course, but the message is clear: if you want your life to be enriched, you need to learn to give—money, time, help. Everyone has *something* to give. Giving can be a joy and givers are players, not just observers.

I've learned not only to take joy in the giving, but also to recognize givers for their community spirit, leadership, and generosity in creating a life-enriching culture.

CHAPTER FIFTEEN

An American Citizen

I'VE ALWAYS LOVED OUR country and consider myself a patriot; however, I've been criticized for speaking out so enthusiastically about freedom, free enterprise, and love of country. In the early days of Amway, with our company name and red, white, and blue logo, some accused us of wrapping ourselves and our products in the American flag. When I was delivering my "Selling America" speech back in the 1970s, patriotism was starting to feel a bit old-fashioned and "corny" to many people. Americans were becoming embarrassed to stand and sing our national anthem before ball games, or self-conscious in placing their hands over their hearts as our flag passed. Some people then and still today question why I am such a gung-ho patriot and fierce defender of our freedoms and free enterprise system. Perhaps they have failed to ever truly appreciate the sacrifices that so many of our earliest citizens made to defend and protect the freedoms we have enjoyed in America since we won our independence and the Founding Fathers signed the Declaration of Independence (pledging their Lives, their Fortunes, and their sacred Honor) and then framed the U.S. Constitution.

It's important to remember that I am of an age group that was called to fight in World War II. Hitler, Stalin, and Tojo were still real to us because we lived during the time when they were around (although Stalin's Russia fought on our side during the war). When I was in high school, Hitler's Luftwaffe was regularly bombing England. It was obvious that his goal was to occupy England and then come across the ocean and defeat America so he could include our country in his growing empire. Hitler was considered our primary enemy, and when the United States was attacked by Japan at Pearl Harbor and then entered the war in Europe as well, England desperately needed our help to protect them from Hitler's threats to their existence.

We discussed, both in school by day and at the dinner table by night, the possibilities of the world being divided up between the Germans and the Japanese. We were well aware that we had to win World War II or lose everything. Every day the newspaper was filled with stories about territories being won, lost, or recovered in Europe or the Pacific, and the United States was seen as being the last defense against tyranny.

During all my years in high school the war raged. I knew that as soon as I turned eighteen I'd be in the service, so I chose to volunteer in the Army Air Corps while still in high school and received my orders to report for duty just three weeks after graduation. Every able-bodied eighteen-year-old male not in a job essential on the home front needed either to volunteer or be drafted.

As I wrote earlier, I was halfway to the ship that was to take me to the Pacific Theater when the war ended—and I ended up on a small island in the Pacific called Tinian, about one hundred miles north of Guam. Because the U.S. base on Tinian was thirteen hundred miles from Tokyo, the U.S. military had designed and built the B-29 bomber specifically to fly the distance from the base there to Tokyo and back. Bombs were loaded onto the B-29s at the Tinian air base for flights to Japan and their hopeful return. Because there were no other islands in the area on which to land if they got in trouble on the way back, we lost some planes and crews.

The United States was planning to invade the Japanese mainland and the base on Tinian was designated as an evacuation post for wounded GIs. However, before the invasion took place, the *Enola Gay* left Tinian with its deadly cargo, and all preparations for the island to receive one hundred thousand American troops who potentially would have been wounded in the invasion became unnecessary. I had been sent there as part of the take-down/clean-up crew.

After the war, during the Cold War between us and the Soviet Union—no longer an ally—Russia was expanding its communist empire. It took over Cuba in 1959, the same year we founded Amway. Our level of concern was very high—especially once it became clear that the Soviets had established nuclear missiles in Cuba that were easily capable of reaching the United States. The Soviet leader at the time, Nikita Khrushchev, warned the United States: "We will bury you."

In addition to the fear of a nuclear attack, some in our country were predicting loudly that free enterprise and the American way were dead, and that communism was about to take over the world. We had watched communism move in the world and knew that these people really had no idea of the true evils of communism or its dictators. But we knew, because we'd been alive to see the destruction and enslavement it had caused.

That's where my patriotism comes from—the firm conviction that we must, at all costs, maintain our freedoms in order to live the kind of life we want. So I began standing up and speaking out and giving my "Selling America" speech to encourage my fellow citizens to believe in and realize the greatness of our country, and to explain the values and virtues of our political and economic system.

Most Americans today were not alive when we fought against dictators who threatened our way of life. Perhaps those threats no longer seem real or immediate to today's citizens, but we who were alive then know better—there is still evil in the world.

I've tried, as a patriotic American, to get involved in supporting political candidates who I believe will best serve the interests of our country and our American way of life. My first significant political involvement was with our then U.S. congressman, Gerald R. Ford. I got to know Jerry Ford quite well because, as the congressman representing our district, he attended just about everything we dedicated in the early days of Amway. We have photos of him as a special guest at major ribbon cuttings. He even joined us to dedicate our first aerosol line. He watched Amway grow, and we worked with him politically during those years. We also worked with Guy Vander Jagt, who was the U.S. congressman representing the district just to the west of Amway. I worked with him to raise money, because Guy was a fund-raiser to help elect more Republicans to Congress. With others, we formed a funding organization called the Republican Congressional Leadership Council (RCLC) to encourage grassroots participation in giving and raising money—we're talking minimum amounts, but they all count up—but more than that, we wanted to generate interest in what was going on in the Republican Party and in politics in general. This was happening during the Reagan era, when George H. W. Bush was the vice president. Vice President and Mrs. Bush were most gracious to entertain the group often during President Reagan's two terms.

Jay and I had supported Ronald Reagan in his presidential runs (although the honest truth was that I first supported Bush in the 1980 primary campaign). Our support didn't come through direct contribution to Reagan's campaign, but through full-page advertisements we ran in popular newsmagazines. As individuals we were not associated with the campaign, but we supported Reagan's free enterprise principles. I recall that we were the only people doing such ads—they were a new political idea in those days. We wanted the Amway distributors and their customers to know that we supported Reagan, in the hope that they would support him, too. That was a fair assumption, and they probably delivered quite a few votes. We also thought the ads might further help Amway distributors recognize the importance of free enterprise to their success.

But it was my association with Guy Vander Jagt that led to my appointment by President Reagan as finance chairman of the Republican National Committee. As I look back on that time, I think I should have asked more questions before accepting the position.

Almost as soon as I said yes, I realized that I was really too busy with Amway to devote the time required—I'd have two full-time jobs. That was the first of two major mistakes I made in the beginning. First, I wasn't a full-timer. Second, when I took over, I suggested two things: that we have a cash bar at our donor meetings (because otherwise the drinks would be paid for from party funds), and that we get rid of the "deadwood" on our payroll (advisors with no specific jobs who were still being paid).

I thought it was crazy for us to be out fund-raising for the Republican Party candidates and then spend so much on ourselves. I really thought it was time to get smart—but neither suggestion went over well. Although it was a generous donor or company that received invitations to events, they typically didn't attend but sent their delegates, who looked forward to being "wined and dined" for free. And the "deadwood" were very much alive and resented having any part of their livelihood cut, whether or not they worked.

When I took over as chairman, I had said, "I've never asked anybody in this government for any favors. I do this work because I believe in what the Republican Party stands for: freedom and free enterprise, and the individual rights of all Americans. Protecting that is my principal motivation." In addition to the above, I had asked to see the finance statements, saying we could raise money more effectively if I knew where it was going. My request was denied.

We also were raising a good bit of money from the smaller givers, and the RCLC members and I wanted to hold events for the small givers, because they were active voters endorsing the party and deserved to be recognized in some way. That never happened, either.

It was a good tour of duty while it lasted and was an education of sorts as well, but when the opposition began to outweigh the support, it was time to resign.

Yet I didn't give up on government or my responsibility as a citizen to serve. I had made some friends in Washington and was gaining support from some in government who appreciated what I stood for. When President Reagan began forming a commission on AIDS, Guy Vander Jagt suggested that I be a member. He was successful in getting my name on the list and apparently it rose to the top with some of the others, and the president appointed us to make up the commission.

Through my service on the AIDS commission and as a fundraiser for the Republican Party, I became quite well acquainted with President Reagan. He used to say a few words to the commission members in the East Room of the White House. I also was able to chat with him several times backstage prior to meetings at which we both spoke.

On the one-year anniversary of Ronald Reagan's inauguration, I chaired a major fund-raiser at the Hilton hotel in Washington, D.C., and as chairman of the event I was in the greenroom with President Reagan and Vice President Bush and their wives. There were just the five of us backstage waiting for President Reagan to go out and address the crowd at this large, sold-out event. He had just been chewed up by one of the national TV news networks and he was really "pissed off" (his words) and still steaming when he arrived in the greenroom. There he was with his wife, Nancy; Vice President and Mrs. Bush; and me, venting. It was a special, behind-the-scenes, off-camera experience with a U.S. president just being himself, something that few people are privileged to witness.

When you get to know U.S. presidents personally and spend time with them behind the scenes, you realize they are just human beings with interests and concerns similar to your own. They are concerned about saving this country and its freedoms, and their focus is to serve the country well. We need more people like that in government.

———

IN 2001, HELEN AND I decided to make a pledge to help launch the National Constitution Center in Philadelphia. As a reporter for the *Philadelphia Inquirer* wrote of our pledge, "their intention was patriotic, not partisan." Since the museum opened, we've given another donation and plan to continue our support. Helping all Americans—especially young people—understand and appreciate our nation's Constitution is important to us. The Constitution Center is another effort in the long struggle to let Americans know how this country came to be and to instill appreciation for all the freedoms we still enjoy. So, the *Inquirer* got it right: our involvement is a gesture of patriotism. We have plenty of partisanship in our government and country right now but in my opinion not enough patriotism.

We need to remind our citizens, as well as those who represent us in government, of our Constitution—what it stands for and what it says. And starting at home, Amway has begun to stimulate in our U.S. distributors a renewed appreciation of free enterprise and American values and principles of government. There was even a meeting for high-achieving Amway distributors at Mount Vernon, the home of George Washington, our first president. The event was hugely successful, and many became more aware of the importance of George Washington's role in the founding of our country, both as a general and a statesman. From its beginning, America has had the world's greatest record of achievement, but the fact that our way of life is not copied by more countries should give us pause. Our responsibility as citizens is to know what's going on—not only what the candidates for whom we're voting stand for regionally and nationally, but what their leanings are in regard to what's going on internationally. We all need to know enough history about what has happened in the world so we as a country won't repeat our mistakes.

People I meet with at the National Constitution Center all know their American history, but too many of us in this country don't. We know too little about its history and why the Founding Fathers who wrote our Constitution said what they did. Many may not, for example, appreciate that George Washington served just two terms as president and then went home, even before the Constitution was amended to limit presidential terms. He believed two terms were enough, and America needed someone else to serve as president after him to show the world that this new country had indeed become a democratic republic, having thrown off the yoke of monarchy. He didn't crave the power of the presidency—he just wanted to serve and then go home.

Since that time our country has grown, the government has expanded, and elected officials have become more eager to go to Washington and less eager to go home when their term is up. Re-election has become the name of the game, and too many of our congressmen have become adept at avoiding taking principled stands on tough issues that might be right for the country but would cost them votes in the next election. They've found being at or near the seat of power so intoxicating that many run for office as long as they can, and remain in Washington even after they're no longer in office. They become lawyers or lobbyists at big firms in Washington because that's where the action is. Working for the people has, for some, become an ego trip that isn't given up very easily.

Jay and I were talking about this one day and concluded that term limits were the answer. We went about forming a committee and got John Eisenhower, brother of the late president Dwight Eisenhower, to become our chairman. The going wasn't easy and we knew it would be particularly tough nationally, but we got term limits passed in a few states. However, states can't determine the election term of a national congressman or senator—that would require a constitutional amendment. So eventually we had to be satisfied with the progress we'd made at the state level.

Living in Washington, D.C., was not cheap then, and it is still expensive. When Jerry Ford was appointed vice president by President Nixon (and although he'd been a congressman for many years) he was broke and looking forward to his first paycheck as vice president to continue his mortgage payments and raise a family of four children who were at or approaching college age. Although he had received a wage large enough to live on, it was not enough to retire on. After his presidency he accepted board jobs in national companies as a source of income. Today serving in the U.S. Congress has become a career with a generous salary plus benefits, but this career depends on staying in office, so a lot of time, energy, and money are spent on being reelected. It's still my feeling that no nationally elected or appointed official should be able to fill a role indefinitely and that every term should have a stated limit.

Congress has passed so many laws and regulations since we began Amway that I doubt anyone today could duplicate what we were able to build. Increased taxes have taken their toll. Our freedoms have in many ways become more limited. Reliance on government handouts has increased and partisanship has invaded almost every area of our lives. No longer are we seen in the world as "the shining city on a hill."

Looking overseas, we see European economies fail because of government debt and overreliance on government services; in the Middle East, some people are fighting to live in a democracy but are being opposed by people who want something quite different; and countries in Africa and elsewhere that have favorable climates, rich natural resources, and citizens who want to be productive are being held back by corrupt dictators and governments.

So how can we in America make the changes necessary to adapt to national and world conditions and still keep our freedom and our liberties intact? There's certainly no easy solution, but we as citizens must be vigilant at all times to prevent any encroachment on the values and freedom we hold dear. We need to be educated, well-informed citizens and voters who choose elected officials who are truly servants of the people, accepting the responsibilities of their office and putting the country's welfare ahead of their own—honest, loyal people of all races and parties, standing shoulder to shoulder to fight for values that are right and true and will serve our country well for generations to come.

CHAPTER SIXTEEN

Hope from My Heart

I'VE BEEN ALIVE FOR the past seventeen years because a renowned heart transplant surgeon in London finally said, "Yes." I needed a heart transplant at age seventy-one to stay alive, but every transplant hospital and surgeon in the United States had turned me down mostly because of my age. I'm alive because of this London surgeon and also because the perfect heart donor for my specific need was found in the nick of time. By the grace of God through answered prayer, I continue to enjoy life in full. God still must have a plan and a purpose for me here on earth.

I believe that's why He spared my life, and I keep living with that in mind.

A few years ago our family held a celebration on the fifteenth anniversary of my heart transplant, and we all were struck by the many grandchildren who still were very young or not yet born when I received my lifesaving operation. Some of them came up to me and said, "I would never have known you, Grandpa." And, more important, from my perspective, I never would have known them and been able to watch them grow and develop as unique individuals.

I also reflect on all that I would not have been able to accomplish during the past years had I not received a new heart. During that period, we built the Helen DeVos Children's Hospital, were donors and fund-raisers for the DeVos Place convention center, and built the JW Marriott hotel in downtown Grand Rapids. The school from which I graduated, Grand Rapids Christian High School, now enjoys the DeVos Center for Arts and Worship auditorium, where for the first time the entire student body can congregate for worship and where students showcase their talents in theater and music.

I also enjoy the fact that in the lobby of that auditorium is a Model A Ford convertible like the one Jay and I used to ride in to that school, which is displayed as a reminder of how our partnership started. Other projects since my transplant include a new sports arena for Hope College, in Holland, Michigan; medical offices on the Medical Mile in Grand Rapids; a building for communications studies at Calvin College, in Grand Rapids; and an exhibit hall in the National Constitution Center. I don't say this to boast, but because it's been so inspiring to realize that I was so close to death, yet God has blessed me with these additional years to work, and I give Him all the glory.

My heart problems actually started many years before I had my heart transplant. I suffered a TIA, a transient ischemic attack, which doctors explained to me was a warning of a possible stroke or heart attack. Taking their advice, I switched to a heart-healthy diet, took medication to reduce my cholesterol level, and exercised daily. Even so, I learned I couldn't reverse or stop my heart disease as it progressed. Sometime after the TIA, I had tests that showed some blockages and was told, "You need to check with your doctor." Instead, I decided to join my kids on a week-end Fourth of July sailboat race across Lake Michigan to Milwaukee. I was working as a crew member, pushing sails around belowdeck, when I felt some chest pains. Realizing I had a problem, I called my doctor when we reached Milwaukee and he said, "Fly home right away—I want to see you."

My doctor, Luis Tomatis, reviewed the results of additional tests and said, "Take off the rest of the holiday weekend, but the day after you'll need surgery to prevent a heart attack."

So he did the surgery and I was fine for the next eight years. But during those eight years my arteries were continuing to suffer further blockage, and in early December 1992 I had a major at-tack. The doctors got me stabilized after a few days, and then I was flown to the Cleveland Clinic to receive a stent, which was then a new technology that very few hospitals were using. It was a Friday evening when I arrived, but Dr. Tomatis was urging the surgeons to operate that night.

The chief surgeon said, "I'll tell you what. I'll operate in the morning . . . if he's still alive."

The operation was successful, but the right side of my heart had already died when I'd had the attack, so I had to be careful about health and activity. I couldn't walk very far without getting exhausted. I had to return periodically to the hospital to have fluids removed from my body because my heart no longer was strong enough to pump fluids through my system. During these visits I'd lose twelve to fifteen pounds of water weight.

Earlier in 1992 I'd had a stroke, so with my energy flagging and my heart condition vastly limiting activity, I resigned as Amway president and asked our son Dick to take my place in the partnership. That also was a blessing, because with Dick in that role I didn't have any additional stress about the future of our business. But I had to accept that suddenly I had some serious limits to the way I lived. I couldn't walk fifty feet without feeling pain and having to sit down.

Dr. Rick McNamara, my cardiologist, would say, "Your heart's gradually failing." By the end of 1996, he and Dr. Tomatis met with Helen and me and said that if I were to live, I needed a heart transplant.

That was a shock. I had been ignoring my condition, stumbling around, not walking much, not doing very much, but still acting as if everything was going to go on as usual. But life was *not* going to go on, and I was confronted with the need for a new heart.

Everything had been prearranged, unknown to me. Dr. Tomatis had called every U.S. transplant center a couple of years earlier to see if they would consider me for a heart. In addition to my age, I had suffered a stroke, had a heart attack, and was diabetic—a very high risk for a transplant. Beyond that, my blood type was a rare AB positive and reduced the number of potential matching donors. But Dr. Tomatis said he knew a heart surgeon in London who would see me. Professor Sir Magdi Yacoub, a thoracic and cardiovascular surgeon at Harefield Hospital, was known for his cutting-edge transplant research and was a highly skilled and respected heart transplant surgeon. Dr. Tomatis said he was my only shot, but that Dr. Yacoub would not agree to take me as a patient until he met with me. Dr. Yacoub had my history and knew my condition, but he still wanted to *see* me first. (My son Dick had already traveled to London to meet him two years earlier, given him my medical history, and urged him to consider me as a transplant candidate.)

I remember announcing to our children and grandchildren just before Christmas that we were going to go to London to try to get a new heart. We couldn't give them any details—all I could do was share what my doctors had told me. But Helen and I were very positive and told everyone, "We're going to London to get a new heart." The Lord gave us so much positivity about it—I'm just amazed when I look back at it today, because there were so many questions. Now that I know the complexity of getting hearts and matches and so forth, I can truly understand how difficult it is for a doctor to tell a patient that they'll get a new heart. Both the doctor and the patient simply have to hope.

When we arrived in London, Dr. Yacoub's first question to me was "Why do you want to live? You've lived a long time," he said. "You've had a full life. Why do you want to live any longer?"

I told Dr. Yacoub, "Well, I've got a great wife, four wonderful kids to live for, and a bunch of grandchildren I'd like to see grow up. I want to do what I can to help them all to flourish."

I now realize that Dr. Yacoub wanted to determine if I had the spirit and strength to endure this major surgery and recovery. Did I have what it took? Did I have support? Did I have family? Did I have people who loved and cared about me, and people I cared about? Because, I learned, that's what it took to get through this operation. Survival depends not just on the condition of your heart but on the condition of your mind— and your faith in God. With family and friends who constantly held me up in prayer, I knew I'd be given the strength I needed.

After this conversation, Dr. Yacoub examined me and listened to my heart, even though he already knew everything he needed to know. Then, looking into my eyes, he said, "Okay, I'll see what I can do." The words we'd been waiting for. I asked the question foremost in my mind: "How long do you think it's going to take to find a donor?"

He said, "I have no idea. It might be a month, next week, tomorrow. It might be six months. You're last on the waiting list after UK citizens. Just stick close. I want you within one hour of the hospital at all times. Come in here once a week for tests that will tell us how you're holding up, to make sure your condition is still good."

So every Monday after that, Helen and I would go to the hospital to meet with our assigned cardiologist, who would supervise the tests, explain to us what each test showed, and basically manage my care. These tests determined that I had insufficient pressure in the right side of my heart. That meant that in addition to needing a donor with my rare blood type, I'd also needed a heart with a strong right side.

The wait for a donor heart began.

Five months passed before we received a phone call from the hospital on a Monday morning suggesting we arrive early for our regular appointment because they might have found a heart for me. The cardiologist who was working with me had become aware of a woman who had come to the hospital for a lung transplant. Not only did this woman share my rare blood type, but her bad lungs had forced her heart to work in such a way that the right side became very strong.

The phone call that morning was because the doctors thought they'd found a donor for her, which could mean a heart for me. In these procedures the donor lungs are typically transplanted along with the donor *heart*, as a single unit, which lessens the possibility of rejection. That meant her heart could be donated to me when a heart-and-lung unit was located for her. She had previously agreed, in such a case, to donate her heart to me. And it looked like that time had come. Helen remembers hearing the helicopter arrive with the heart and lungs the woman needed. After the doctors had received and approved them, she was put in one operating room to receive new lungs and a heart, and I was in the next OR to have her heart transplanted into me.

I was told her heart was only out of body about twenty to thirty minutes until it was beating in my chest, and it has been doing well for me ever since. People later would remark, "It must have been hard waiting for a heart." But Helen and I would read our favorite verses in Philippians chapter 4 every morning and move forward with confidence and peace.

I know it might be hard to believe, but Helen and I never really had a down day. We truly believed that "God's timing is perfect and He makes no mistakes." Even though I was getting weaker, we stayed pretty busy. At least one of our children was always with us—sometimes with their spouse or their whole family.

It's difficult to describe how elated we were on that Monday morning when the hospital called with the news that there might be a heart for me. We felt a mix of emotions on the way to the hospital—relief, excitement, hope, and joy. When we arrived at the hospital they said, "Everything's a go. We're going to prep you for surgery."

First I was given a shot, which I'm sure contained something for anxiety because I started to feel pretty good considering the fact I was about to go into major surgery. I remember that, on a gurney heading for the operating room, I was being wheeled past one of the cardiologists who had gray hair that stuck straight up, the one I had always kidded about needing a haircut. As I passed him, I sat up on the gurney and teased him one more time, "Hey, Doc, you need a haircut!"

After the surgery, when I awoke momentarily from the anesthesia, I saw some of my family at my bedside. The boys remember one of the first things I said was "Let's thank God." And I prayed a prayer of praise and thanksgiving and glory to Him. I don't remember it at all. But that prayer must have come from deep in my soul because when I realized, even fleetingly, that I was still alive the first thing I did was thank God.

The rest of the family was on their way to London and Mid-Atlantic gathered inside the plane, all of them on their knees, and prayed together for a successful outcome. When they landed they received word that the surgery had gone well and arrived at the hospital toward the end of the surgery. Dr. Tomatis came on that flight and stuck right with me for the whole time. He was there every day to encourage me. So was Dr. McNamara. When the hospital let Dr. McNamara examine my old heart, he said, "It was so dead. I couldn't believe it kept you alive at all."

The worst part of the recovery was the medication I was given to prevent my body from rejecting the new heart. The doses were heavy in the days immediately after surgery and made me have frightening and bizarre nightmares. At night I would dream all sorts of things. I once saw myself as a pygmy, in Grand Rapids, down by the old Rowe Hotel next to the Grand River. I was just a little person because I didn't have any legs. I remember reaching down in the bed to make sure they were still there. The next day I actually asked someone to come to my bed and check again!

Another time I saw myself in a cardboard box, oddly enough, near our house in Florida, floating north. I had a telephone, and there I was, bobbing along in the Gulf Stream, calling for help, saying that I was being carried away from the shore. These nightmares were very scary and seemed very real. In fact they were so unnerving that I would do anything I could to avoid going to sleep. I would get in the wheelchair and ask to be pushed around the hospital, just to stay awake.

One day I was lying in bed when Dr. Yacoub came by. Seeing me there, he asked sharply, "What are you doing in bed?"

I told him I didn't know—I must be tired or something.

"Get out of bed," he said. "I took a chance on you. You were a high-risk patient. I took a chance on doing this and hoped you could make it."

I said, "Thank goodness."

He said, "Act like it. You have no reason to lie around anymore, other than your own fear. You can do anything you want. Get up and get going."

That was a challenge, a good one. I was still thinking of myself as having a heart problem but he wanted me to realize that I had a new heart now and could do whatever I wanted to do. I must have gotten a little depressed after a couple of weeks recovering in the hospital, but when Dr. Yacoub challenged me to get up, I decided I had to get up and get going. That was a good zinger for me that day.

I had also developed a fear of rejection of the new organ by my body. At first I was kind of uptight about it. After the wait and long odds, after finding a heart and surviving the surgery, I was afraid that after coming so far it all could be ended by my body rejecting my new heart. I couldn't sleep the night before I was scheduled for a biopsy to test for signs of rejection. I even tried to watch as the doctor snipped tissue from my heart.

"What are you looking for?" he asked.

"I want to see if that piece of tissue you just took out of me is brown instead of red."

He said, "Actually, you don't want it to be *white*. If it's white, you know you have a problem. White means there's no blood in the tissue."

I was tested like this once a week at first and then every other week. Thankfully, I've never had a rejection problem, but I'll still need to take my anti-rejection medication for the rest of my life.

Harefield Hospital was built in the World War I era and was originally a tuberculosis sanitarium. The hospital runs along a street and curves in and out to allow the air in each room to blow in a front window and out a back window, so it's one room wide and curved like a serpent. When they added indoor plumbing, the bathrooms were built across from some of the rooms but seemed to me to be about a quarter mile apart.

Shortly after I got my heart, I was taking the long walk down the hall toward the bathroom when a woman patient popped out of a door and asked me, "Did you get your heart last Tuesday?"

And I said, "Yes, I did."

She said, "You have *my* heart."

So I said, "Thank you!" and gave her a hug. We saw each other a few times during our hospital stay, and then I saw her again when I got my ten-year checkup. I understand she died of cancer a year or two later. She had wanted to be a singer and dreamed of making a recording, and I was able to help her do that. She was a nice lady. But I knew little of her life story and never got to know her as we both moved on with our lives in different countries.

Another remarkable result of my heart transplant is that we were able to build relationships with some of the greatest heart surgeons in the world and bring them to our hospitals in Grand Rapids. Dr. Yacoub was mandated to retire from the National Health Service in Britain at age sixty-five. He's brilliant and still has so much to offer, and is now serving in a consulting capacity to the transplant unit at the Meijer Heart Center at Spectrum Hospital. He remains the leading heart transplant surgeon in the world, both in a research capacity and also because of the number of transplants he has performed.

In the early days of transplantation, when many hearts were available and many people were on the list to receive them, he and his partner, Dr. Asghar Khaghani, would perform three transplants a day. They told us that they'd do a transplant, take a nap, and then scrub the operating room for the next surgery. Now Dr. Yacoub visits Grand Rapids's transplant center a couple of times a year and Dr. Khaghani now heads up that center. One of their associates from England is now on the staff at our children's hospital—he's recognized as one of the best in the world, and we're blessed to have him. Through these doctors' influence, other specialists have joined our hospital staff, each one enriching not only our hospital system, but the whole community as well.

I'm grateful for my successful heart transplant and for all the things God has helped me accomplish since then. And I'm both amazed at and thankful for the ripple effect that experience has had for me, my family, and my community.

CHAPTER SEVENTEEN

Adventures in God's World

A S MY HEART GREW weaker while awaiting a transplant in London, I remained positive and optimistic about the future. With no guarantee of a new lease on life, I still had a dream—I guess that was part of my nature. Even my serious heart condition could not stop me from dreaming and having goals and projects. They kept me moving forward and helped me focus on the positive versus worrying about the negatives in life.

So while I was waiting for a new heart I went ahead with work on my latest dream—to sail around the world. Instead of worrying about what might happen in my health situation, I kept occupied by designing a new sailboat. My plans for that boat to sail around the world helped me keep a positive outlook but also led to the realization of a new and great adventure.

During my five-month wait for a heart, I was thinking about this boat, the interior layout, the number of staterooms, the sail combinations, type, and manufacturer. Our captain would visit me in London, and we would discuss ideas and write down our specifications for the boat as well as the best routing and timing for our around-the-world trip. Each week as different members of our family came to visit, we also talked with them about progress on the boat design, so they also had a chance to enjoy the process.

At one point I made the comment to my son Doug, "After all this work, I may never live to use this boat." He replied jokingly, "That's okay. Your kids will use it." Instead of impatiently and nervously waiting for a heart, I was actually busy designing this boat and peacefully dreaming of South Pacific voyages.

The boat was mostly completed by the time I got out of the hospital after my transplant, so we arranged for a big party on deck at the shipyard. An airplane load of people came from Grand Rapids and we invited some other friends from Europe to be our guests as we launched the boat in Viareggio, Italy.

The boat turned out magnificently. We christened her *Independence*. She was a ketch, meaning there was a mainmast forward and about halfway back a second mast that's a bit shorter. With a mainsail, aft sail, and a jib sail at the front, *Independence* could reach speeds exceeding ten knots, which is fast for a sail-boat. The sails were huge but all were self-furling and raised and lowered within ten minutes by electric winches at the push of buttons. While *Independence* was a beautiful boat, the real beauty of owning such a sailboat is the opportunity it provides to sail almost anywhere in the world. Our trip took us from Italy to the Caribbean, then through the Panama Canal and into the Galapagos Islands before sailing across the South Pacific into the Marquesas. They're just a speck on the map but a beautiful, re-mote group of French islands. From there, we'd go farther south to Tahiti and Bora Bora, islands in the French Polynesian group. *Independence* had a crew of ten, including the captain and his first mate; two stewardesses; a chef; and deckhands, who cleaned the boat, washed off the salt every day, and drove the tenders that took us ashore or wherever else we wanted to go. My three sons and I all know how to drive boats, so we would take our turns at the helm. *Independence* also had twelve bunks, so we could always have family and friends along for different legs of our voyage.

Our family has fallen in love with the South Pacific and its isolated islands. Many of these settings are ideal for children, with calm, clear lagoons for swimming. The lagoons have inlets from the ocean through which boats can pass and then anchor in the calm waters protected from the big waves of the Pacific.

In the Marquesas, for example, our children and grandchil-dren swam in a big round lagoon of shallow water with several outlets in the ocean. The water would pour out of those inlets when the tide went down. At low tide, some of the older children, in scuba gear, would hang on to an inlet wall and watch sharks at the mouth of the outlet waiting for fish to flow into the ocean. Our children loved to scuba and snorkel in this crystal-clear water of the South Pacific. Early in our Pacific sailings Helen learned to snorkel and fondly remembers bobbing on the surface and being able to see some of her children and grandchildren below her in their scuba gear. She may also have been a bit concerned because on the ocean floor were a few small sharks, but we never had an incident.

We also met and befriended fellow travelers who had been sailing great distances for weeks or sometimes months. We would be anchored in the same lagoons or docked in the same ports and visit each other's boats. Someone might sail by some evening and say, "Potluck on our boat!" and everybody who wanted to would go over to their boat bearing some food, and share dinners and stories and get acquainted with people from all over the world. They were sailing oftentimes with two people or maybe three—just small crews on small boats.

Our boat was pretty big in comparison to most of the ocean sailors we met. We were sometimes their water or ice supplier, because many of these smaller boats didn't have generators or equipment for making drinking water or ice. We met many people this way, chatted with them at night, or had them over for something to drink and heard about their adventures. We learned why they were on their voyages and what got them going on the idea of sailing across such vast expanses of water.

One of *Indy*'s longest runs was from the Galapagos to the Marquesas. That's three thousand miles with no stopping in between, a voyage of about two weeks. On the short stretches between islands we kept busy with watching movies or playing games or reading books. Breakfast was on our own, but we ate lunch and dinner together. I would sit between two of our grandchildren and give them a few words of advice that they may have needed but didn't always want to hear. It was a nice family time together on a trip that included doing things they had never done or thought of before.

For most of our stops we furled our sails and dropped anchor. Few places had docks, so we'd anchor and use our dinghy to go ashore. We were usually greeted by the native islanders. In Fiji we needed clearance from the island chief to come ashore and would be expected to bring him a gift of tobacco and kava root. He'd have the kava pulverized, then someone would put the powder inside a cloth bag and squeeze it by hand through a bowl of water as often as necessary. The result is a drink that numbs the tongue and lips and makes the drinker sleepy—it is their replacement drink for alcohol.

As we arrived ashore in the Fijian islands, the chief would greet us. He was the official greeter and the one who checked our papers. (We needed a letter from the president of Fiji to go to some of the islands.) We visited some of the outer islands in the easternmost part of the Fijian group that are off-limits to cruising boats, unless they have applied for a special document from the president. Fiji tries to limit tourism on these islands to protect their culture. We had been to the country's capital and secured our letter.

These islands are in the middle of a big ocean. I said to one Fijian native, "How many boats did you have visit this year?"

He said, "Oh, we've had quite a few."

I said, "Really? How many, would you say?"

He said, "Three."

It was interesting to see the children go to school, dressed in their uniforms, heading for the "school boat." While the younger children were taught on-island, the older students attended a "consolidated" school on a nearby island.

Fijian islanders, although very isolated, are as friendly as can be. They speak English, since originally Fiji was an English colony, so we were able to converse with and get to know them as we spent time on their islands. We got to know their needs and asked guests who were joining us for a portion of the trip to bring any old clothing or shoes they no longer wore or that their children had outgrown. They responded generously, and when we went ashore it was like Christmas. The bags emptied rapidly and all the items were shared; whenever we returned we would see these clothes being worn, and that made us smile.

Sometimes we were invited over to share a meal, which was a very special treat. The first time we were invited was for a Sunday dinner after church. When we arrived, the meal was hot and ready, since it had been cooking all during church in the stone oven our hosts had fashioned in the ground behind their house. Dessert was the sweet milk we drank from a coconut opened by a machete.

The second time was on a visit to Fulaga. We anchored close because we'd heard the people there did wood carving and we were always interested in seeing and often buying pieces of native art. So we piled into the dinghy, wallets ready. Our group found much there to take home and, as a gesture of thanks, we were invited to remain on the island for dinner.

As it turned out, dinner was a cooperative affair in what looked to be their "community center"—basically a roof and a floor. First we watched as one of the women carefully laid a colorful rectangular piece of fabric on the floor. That, we discovered, was the tablecloth. When it was time, the right people were called to join our family, and we all sat around the tablecloth. Pots of food were brought. We were invited to eat but didn't see any forks, so we held back to see what the natives did. They dove right in and helped themselves to the food with their fingers, eating it directly from their hands. When they realized we were unfamiliar with their ways, someone gathered up a few unmatched plates and forks so we could eat. Mostly we ate food they'd grown and fish they'd caught—although we didn't recognize any of the food. It was a fascinating time spent with wonderful, generous people, and it became one of our favorite cross-cultural adventures.

About five hundred miles to the east of Fulaga is a group of islands called the Lau group, and upon arrival an "emissary" told us that the chief wanted to see us. We hurried to go ashore to find him. That was unusual—had we done something wrong?

"You haven't checked in with me" was his unusual greeting.

"There are other chiefs on this island, two smaller villages with chiefs, but I am the main chief, my village is the largest, and you haven't cleared with me."

We had attended church on one of the islands and given generously. It seemed the preacher of that church also came from this chief's island, so word had apparently spread about our contributions, and clearly this chief wanted a share for his people.

In the town square of each village is a church, and the village is built around the church. On Sunday morning everyone gets dressed up. The people are poor, but all the men have ties and wear neatly pressed white shirts. The pastor wears a suit jacket along with his *sulu,* which all men wear, and is best described as a wraparound skirt that reaches just below his knees. The women and children are all dressed up as well. Once a family enters the church, the school-age boys sit together in the pews on the left and the rest of the family sits together elsewhere.

The singing of the choirs is just awesome. And there's an "enforcer," a male member who walks up and down the aisles carrying a long stick. If any kids are whispering or have fallen asleep, he reaches in from the aisle and taps them with his stick. They also keep track of the offerings at collection time. Their privileged members, when called by name, walk down the center aisle to where a table has been quietly set up and give their offering—which is duly noted by the treasurer seated at the table, in his ledger. They ask the tourists to respond, and so then we all give.

Our friends would ask, "How much do I give?" I'd say, "You can't give too much. They're poor. If you feel like giving a hundred dollars, give 'em a hundred dollars. You might never be here again." The Fijians never forgot us, because I always, when I met the chief, would give him a hundred dollars or more for his church. He would receive it, check the amount, and pass it to the person on his right, who also checked it out and passed it to a third person—all this to let us know it would go where it belonged. If we invited them aboard *Indy,* they were interested to see it and were always respectful, but they never showed a bit of jealousy for what they saw. They seemed very happy and content with their way of life.

Our family loves the Pacific for its natural beauty and the friendliness of the people. We visited Fiji three different times and revisited many of the same islands, and thus some of the people recognized our boat and saw when we were arriving. They would welcome us and ask, "Will you be coming to visit *our* village?" Often we would return there on another cruise and we'd see snapshots we'd taken and given to them earlier hanging on a wall, or a colorful page from a magazine we'd left for them. They loved the magazines we left behind—if they didn't read them, they still put them to use.

As I look back on these sailing trips, I realize how advanced America is compared to many other parts of the world. The South Pacific has a fairly simple island economy. Getting water and food is a struggle. But the people are very hospitable, and by spending time on these islands, I learned that each has its own unique charm. "Bula vinaka" is the traditional Fijian greeting. It's easy for visitors to learn and it seems to work for any occasion.

––––

AFTER MAKING OUR WAY across the top of Australia, we sailed into the Indian Ocean and west to the Seychelles, beautiful islands off the east coast of Africa with a capital city and a good airport. We also ventured to Cape Town, South Africa, sailing around the Cape of Good Hope, which has long been known among sailors for its rough weather. Winds come up off Antarctica at about sixty to seventy miles per hour every four days. Even when we were tied up in Cape Town harbor, some nights winds would reach a gale force of sixty miles per hour and would make *Indy* heel noticeably. One night, with winds blowing at this velocity and our boat heeling in its slip, I remember the movie we happened to be watching was *The Perfect Storm*.

––––

OUR CRUISE ON *INDY* confirmed my lifelong belief in adventure and also the value of experiencing places far from home and people of different cultures. Going back as far as my trip with Jay to Montana as boys and then traveling together through South America, I recall how these experiences opened our hearts and minds.

When Jay and I drove to Nutrilite in California in the early days, we would stop in the mountains to ski, a new experience for me. We tested our abilities and resolve on our sailing adventure. As a young father, I encouraged our family to travel to experience unfamiliar places in the world. I also think back to my father's curiosity and sense of adventure as he looked on maps at places he could only dream of visiting. I feel very fortunate that I have actually realized his adventures.

Adventure teaches us about possibilities we may never have imagined, helps us gain confidence in our abilities, and encourages us to recognize that even people who live differently from us are really no different in their needs and aspirations than we are. We all share the same planet and owe it to ourselves and others to be curious about the world, share our cultures and experiences, and stand in awesome wonder at God's creation.

We made friends with people in Fiji, and even though we were prosperous Americans visiting on a large sailboat, we could enjoy a worship service and Sunday dinner with these people of simple means. It turns out that despite their simple means, they enjoy a richness of life.

Reflecting on this sailing adventure, I'm struck by the size of our world, and the isolation and beauty of nature. I feel very blessed to be able to have experienced such wonders. In a huge ocean, beneath hundreds of stars, where islands are just dots on a map, there is a spiritual dimension to what you experience. I continue to marvel at this wonderful world and all the people in it. In our civilized life, we get so wrapped up in schedules and our dependence on technology, living in homes with all sorts of conveniences, and too few people have the opportunity or even the desire to experience and appreciate our world's vastness, its beauty, and the sheer pleasure of the solitude and silence that can come while on water. I was fascinated to meet people who lived for the adventure of being on their own in small boats in a huge ocean. Not many people today voluntarily step out of their comfort zone to experience an adventure beyond their daily routine. I believe the people who do are the kind with the initiative and daring that keep us progressing as a society and civilization.

CHAPTER EIGHTEEN

Promises to Keep

AMWAY AND ITS RELATED companies reported sales for 2012 of $11.3 billion, our seventh consecutive year of sales growth. Our largest markets are many that once were communist regimes—China, Ukraine, and Russia—and were never dreamed of as one day having free economic opportunities. In 2013, Amway started construction of new manufacturing plants in the United States, China, India, and Vietnam. Today NUTRILITE is the world's number-one-selling vitamin and dietary supplement brand and accounts for 46 percent of Amway's business.

Despite such overwhelming success, we still have a few critics who fail to understand our way of business. That's why I'm so indebted to all the distributors who have stuck by us over the years—our early Nutrilite group who came on board when Jay and I started Amway, distributors who remained dedicated through the Canadian and FTC cases and all the negative publicity, and people around the world who joined us despite some suspicion by their governments.

Today hundreds of them are millionaires, thousands are successful business owners, and hundreds of thousands are earning additional income to help themselves and their families; they have taken responsibility for their lives, benefiting from a positive attitude and the hope of fulfilling their potential through a free-market opportunity. Millions of people worldwide now have an opportunity that all began with two young guys who simply recognized the potential of people, and saw in the human spirit an inherent longing to reach out for "something better."

Phrases such as "could never have dreamed" or "beyond our wildest imagination" cannot begin to describe where things stood just fifty years ago and how this phenomenon has exploded. I'm proud that Jay and I, from the beginning, focused our efforts on helping people and giving them an opportunity. That continues to be the secret of Amway's international success today.

As I look back, I believe the one word that describes my feelings is *thankful*. I remain thankful not only that God has blessed our business success, but also for the success of my family; for having been born in America with its blessings of freedom; for my Christian faith; and for influences that have taught me to see the dignity in each person, to be accountable, to experience the rewards of hard work, and to realize the power of persistence and unlimited potential.

These have been my lifetime beliefs, and I have never wavered.

These are my concrete values not because I am stubborn or have never considered other points of view. These are simply the principles that have proven over time to be my foundation for a successful, fulfilling, and joyful life—a life that not only has been rewarding to me but has resulted in rewards for many others. I am tolerant of other beliefs, but I simply cannot argue with the guidelines that have proven true for me.

Thinking back to my youth as related in the first chapter of this book, I think about how grateful I am to have grown up in a two-parent home with two sisters, and the support of family: grandparents, cousins, and relatives. All our relatives were employed and didn't even think to wait around for unemployment help. I didn't know about government assistance or any other means of receiving income. My home was where I was taught and encouraged to work and get educated. It was there I was taught principles of hard work, where I was exposed to a father who was always fixing things and doing things, and urging me to be in business for myself.

Then I met a kid who had been taught the same thing and shared a similar background, so we teamed up. Some people are born with talents but never develop them. Maybe they fought with their mother instead of listening when she said, "Study tonight!" But only those who learn to value *work* and *education* succeed.

It comes back to parenting and home and attitude. God blessed me to be born in the right home with two parents and an extended family with a history of being hard workers, going back to my grandfathers, who both immigrated to this country because they wanted to get ahead and provide a better opportunity for the children they hoped to raise.

As the father of four, grandfather of sixteen, and great-grandfather of two, I'm still most gratified in life by home and family. My first house with Helen was the one we built on a hill overlooking a river. Although this house has changed to meet our needs over the years, it's still home, where we grew together and where we raised our family. When the kids are around, they drop in, and even with the changes they still consider this house as the home they grew up in, and it's been home to Helen and me for more than sixty years.

Building a successful family, of course, begins with a successful marriage. In February 2013, Helen and I celebrated our sixtieth wedding anniversary, and the years have been good to us. I think back to the early years of our courtship and believe I was a bit reckless and too casual. We just dated off and on—I think Helen found me a bit too outspoken and forward. Yet we kept coming together. But I think about what a blessing she has been, and how I took those early years for granted. Our marriage was going the way marriages should go; we had four healthy babies.

Over the years we became more aware and realized how truly blessed we are—when you're young, you are unaware of all the blessings you have!

Our kids have grown up well, married, and blessed us with sixteen grandchildren. And now we even have great-grandchildren. Our two-year-old great-granddaughter jumps on my lap and calls me Grandpa Great. Maybe others can't understand what she's saying, but I can!

I also simply expect Amway to keep growing. Maybe it's not just the young who take things for granted! I recently was reminded that Amway is *required* to grow. A member at a board meeting proposed changing operations to save millions of dollars on shipping costs. I said flippantly, "I don't care. I don't need any more money."

"Right," he said, "but I do." It was a great line. He needed Amway to flourish so he could do likewise. I said, "Yes, sir. You're right. I'm wrong." We have to be strong and profitable for the people coming up. If we don't grow, they don't have any added chance to go ahead, salaries are stagnant, and opportunities decrease. So it's important that we grow today for tomorrow's employees and distributors. Distributors who start today have to know that we will be here for them—that they have the same opportunity. I've told my children, "You will always have to be running this business in a growth mode." Amway's still an important part of my life—thinking about it, going to events, and speaking periodically. I like that.

I also continue my interests beyond Amway. In support of

my love of America and free enterprise, I'm working with various groups that are trying to find a way to make this a better and more prosperous country for more people. As with Amway, the country needs to grow. If the country doesn't grow, the American people don't grow. Many people don't think in those terms. They're complacent and happy with where things stand today. But that's not good enough; it'll just kill everything for the next generation coming up. That idea closely parallels Amway. We need opportunity for individuals to grow and prosper, and to encourage others to do the same.

That's true for our country, our churches, and our businesses. The only way to increase the wealth of the nation is to increase the business of the nation. That makes more wealth available. Socialism has *never* worked in all of history, so why are we trying to force this country to go down that path? It doesn't make any sense. I want my country to follow a good success pattern and am working with others who want to achieve that same goal.

My Christian faith and outreach also remain strong after all these years. The Christian church and Christian education are high on our list of giving. Helen and I are mostly focused on Christian, community, political, and national projects. Our family foundations remain heavily involved in providing funding for worthy causes. Collectively, our family has given away millions, but if the government increases our taxes by a big number, that makes it tough to have that number to give away. If the government takes it, then I can't give it—and I enjoy giving. *My* giving it puts the money into better hands than the government's.

I'm still working on the effort to reunite the Reformed Church in America and Christian Reformed Churches, and since many have agreed with the idea, it has now become their project as well. Several churches and organizations are pursuing unification. I also want to help turn around other churches both in America and in the world beyond. Christians are losing the ability to witness as churches fail and die. The number of people accepting salvation through Christ is not growing, and yet that is the principal responsibility of the church. We're not doing a very good job of it.

Many leaders in the church see the numbers dwindling and say they are not good at bringing in new members. I tell them, "You'd better become good at it or the church will die." If an Amway group didn't continue to add members, I would tell them they were going to fail. That's the same challenge facing our churches.

––––

I'M STILL TRYING IN my lifetime role as cheerleader and encourager to have a positive influence on my grandchildren and great-grandchildren. They are the future, and as an eternal optimist, I believe that today's young people have the capacity to build a successful future, but they need guidance from those of us who have succeeded in the past. I've seen how Amway, for example, has helped people teach their children how to work. A lot of the kids whose parents are involved in Amway are learning how to put on a meeting or to help to greet people at the door. Some who did this early on are now second-generation distributors, and there are third-generation distributors just around the corner. They are in families that talk about these things and consider them important to their children's growth.

I'm also encouraging my grandchildren to get a better education than I had by completing work for a college degree and even an advanced degree. They will need to compete at a higher level. I told one of my granddaughters that she needed to finish college to be in the same category as her siblings and cousins. She said jokingly, "Grandpa, what do you know about it? You didn't go to college." I said, "That's why I know it's important!" We now have grandchildren in medical and law schools at leading Michigan universities, and others who have or are completing their bachelor's degrees.

Helen and I have relationships with all of our grandchildren, and now and then they look to me for a little guidance and encouragement, because if I am anything, I am their encourager. Starting a business, starting a life of your own, or starting a family—it all takes a lot of strength and courage. You've got to really apply yourself and work at it consistently and persistently.

Parents need to work at helping children learn accountability and the value of work. We need to take an interest in our children, teaching them how to communicate, seeing that they get the right education, and helping them be aware of where they're at in life. We need to be aware who their friends are and where they go every day, make sure they do their homework, and dedicate ourselves to helping them grow to be the best they can be.

Just getting to know them is half the game. I was speaking to a group in Florida one night when some started mentioning that their grandchildren did not call them enough. I said, "How many of you call your grandchildren?" I got a dead silence. I said, "Telephones work both ways, you know." Grandchildren are busy, just as we think we're busy. It's not always easy for them to stay in touch. I usually just pick up the phone and call, but children these days can be hard to reach because they don't even answer their phones anymore. Do we need to learn to text if we want to get a message through? I try, but my fingers are too big! Those are just excuses for not working harder at it, so I still pick up the phone and call.

Sooner or later I get through.

I've made a lot of promises over the years and have dedicated my life to trying to keep them. During the darkest days of World War II, as president of my senior class I gave a speech at graduation that expressed an optimistic view of America's future. I promised Jay that we would stick together as friends and business partners. I vowed to Helen to be her faithful husband for life. Jay and I asked people to believe in our unusual Nutrilite business and products and then join us as we started a new business called Amway. In speeches I touted with unflagging confidence the promise of free enterprise and the American way. I took to heart my father's sincere lecture about the promises I had to keep to employees and distributors as Amway started to grow.

I still must live up to my promise to millions of people worldwide that Amway will continue to grow and provide them a continuing opportunity for success, a promise in which my family has since joined me. I felt comfortable making these promises because I've always been the eternal optimist, filled with hope.

So much of my success in life depended on keeping promises. And promises only can be made and kept from a foundation of truths that guide our lives and cannot be shaken by changing circumstances. As the old saying goes, "What is popular is not always right, and what is right is not always popular." I've tried to do what is right regardless of critics, changing lifestyles, the party in power, or those whose views or influence might hold sway in society at any given time. Opinions, trends, and fads come and go. But I've never been able to argue against the wisdom of having an upward look, being persistent, believing in America and free enterprise, a Christian faith and a loving family, being accountable to myself and others, and recognizing the dignity in each person.

These are all such simple beliefs and values that have helped people lead successful lives for many years. But unfortunately, they are no longer so obvious to many people. I feel very blessed that God has instilled these truths in my life and put me in positions to learn them and experience their power. I'm most thankful that through these blessings I've been able to help so many people around the world help themselves and experience the fullness of life that God intended for them. I guess that's why He made me a cheerleader who saw my mission in life as seeing the best in people and encouraging them.

In planning a tribute to me recently, my family asked friends of mine to offer stories that best illustrated who I am as a person. I was touched by all these stories, but especially the following one offered by my friend and doctor, Luis Tomatis, and told by one of my grandchildren at the tribute:

"Grandpa and Dr. Tomatis traveled to Washington, D.C., to meet with the secretary of health for a discussion about increasing organ donations. The day was snowy. Security was tight shortly after Nine-Eleven. They were not allowed to park any closer than a half mile from the building and had to walk the rest of the way. They got on the elevator in the lobby with many other people who all were commenting on the bad weather and how they had to walk in the snow. One person on the elevator was in an electric wheelchair. As everyone was joking about the weather, he commented that in such weather his wheelchair really should have a windshield with windshield wipers.

"Once off the elevator, they were walking down the hallway, when Grandpa turned to the man in the wheelchair and noticed that his glasses were still wet from the melting snow. Realizing the man was a quadriplegic and unable to remove his glasses, Grandpa offered to clean them for him. He took a handkerchief from his pocket and carefully wiped the man's glasses dry. He then put the glasses back on the man's face, and with his index finger carefully pressed the glasses securely in place. 'Is that all right?' Grandpa asked, to which this paralyzed man in the wheelchair said, 'Yes. Thank you.'

"Dr. Tomatis later recalled: 'Here I was, a doctor, and we also had a security person with us, but we never realized the man was a quadriplegic or took notice of his need or offered to help. Rich not only noticed, but quickly sized up this person's predicament, and took a loving approach to help a fellow human being in need.'"

I was blessed with a love for people and know that seeing the best in people, recognizing them as fellow children of God, getting to know them as unique individuals, and believing in them has been a key to success in Amway. And also, I believe, to the success of families, our country, our communities, and to life itself!

I leave you with two phrases that have been keys to my success: "Be a Life Enricher" and "You Can Do It!"